D1270109

NICOLO PAGANINI:
HIS LIFE AND WORK.

Plate I.—See Appendix.

PORTRAIT OF NICOLO PAGANINI BY MAURIN.

NICOLO PAGANINI:

HIS LIFE AND WORK,

BY

STEPHEN S. STRATTON.

———

" Natura il fece, e poi ruppe la stampa."
ARIOSTO.

WITH TWENTY-SEVEN ILLUSTRATIONS.

GREENWOOD PRESS, PUBLISHERS
WESTPORT, CONNECTICUT

Originally published in 1907
by The Strad Office, London and
Charles Scribner's Sons, New York

First Greenwood Reprinting 1971

Library of Congress Catalogue Card Number 75-109856

SBN 8371-4347-0

Printed in the United States of America

PREFACE.

THE author of this work did not live to see the final
sheets in print. Although it has not received his revision,
yet the book has had careful editing. Mr. Stratton did
not undertake the Life of Paganini without adequate
preparation. He had during many years thoughtfully
studied the artist and his attributes, and became an
acknowledged authority on the subject. He gathered
from all available sources the most reliable information.
Almost his last journey was a pilgrimage to Paganini's
birthplace. This volume will exhibit his versatility,
particularly the chapter giving the analyses of Paganini's
compositions. It is therefore the most complete account of
the greatest virtuoso recorded in the annals of music.
Those who peruse this most interesting biography of
Paganini, will naturally desire to learn something of the
writer.

Stephen Samuel Stratton was born in London on
December 19th, 1840. He began his career as a chorister
of St. Mary's Church, Ealing. He studied harmony and
composition under Charles Lucas. As an organist, he
held these appointments—St. Mary the Virgin, Soho ; and
St. James's Church, Friern Barnet. On his removal to
Birmingham in 1866, he was organist at St. Barnabas
Church ; Edgbaston Old Parish Church ; St. John's,

Harborne; and the Church of the Saviour (1878-1882). In 1879 he commenced a series of chamber concerts in Birmingham.

From 1877 until the day of his death, Mr. Stratton was the musical critic of the "Birmingham Daily Post." In that position his influence was decidedly beneficial. He was also a contributor to the London Musica Press. He will be remembered as the joint author (with Mr. James D. Brown) of "British Musical Biography." His "Life of Mendelssohn" was written for Messrs. Dent's "Master Musicians." Among other items may be mentioned "Musical Curiosities," and valuable papers read before the "Incorporated Society of Musicians."

In private life he was highly esteemed—an honorable citizen—a genial, kind hearted man, with a genuine love of his profession. He died, after a short illness, in Birmingham, on June 25th, 1906.

R. H.

CONTENTS.

CONTENTS.

CHAPTER X.

NICOLO PAGANINI:

HIS LIFE AND WORK.

CHAPTER I.

THERE are some names, the mere mention or thought of which conjure up distinct personalities; such are Handel, Bach, Beethoven, Wagner; but not one has the extraordinary individuality of that of Paganini. Though few can be living who ever saw the man, though his portraits are not now commonly to be met with, the name of Paganini at once calls up a picture—weird, uncanny, demoniacal; brings back the faint echo of performances long lost in the corridors of time; and excites the imagination in a manner altogether unique. The last few years have witnessed the appearance of an unprecedented number of wonderful young violinists, whose achievements culminate in the marvellous playing of the boy Franz von Vecsey. These manifestations are almost enough to induce belief in the theory or doctrine of reincarnation, and to make one fancy that the great Genoese is once again in the flesh. These violinists, too, are all playing Paganini's music; they seem to glory in it, and so do the audiences, although

to many serious and worthy folk it is mere clap-trap
stuff. This revived interest in Paganini and his music
seems to render the present an appropriate time to
restate the case of the man and the artist, notwithstanding the extensive literature already associated with
his name.

It is a curious fact that nearly every distinguished
musician, composer or executant, has his namesakes.
There was a constant succession of Bachs in Thuringia
for nearly two centuries; Beethoven's father and grand-
father were musicians; there were four Mozarts,
musicians; and more than twenty Wagners of some
standing in the musical world. No one seems to have
traced the pedigree of Paganini, but he was preceded and
followed by others bearing the same name, and such
particulars as can be gleaned concerning these Paganinis
may not be without interest, and at least may serve by
way of introduction to the greatest of them all.

Dr. Burney, in his account of Italian Opera in London
during the last half of the eighteenth century, names a
Signor and Signora Paganini as engaged for the season
of 1760-61. They came from Berlin, and the Doctor is
ungallant enough to say that the lady, known as " The
Paganini," was not young. She made her *début* on
November 22, 1760, in Galuppi's " Il Mondo della Luna,"
in a *buffa* part, and was very captivating. At her benefit,
when another opera by Galuppi was given—" Il Filosofo
di Campagna,"—such a crowd assembled as had never
been seen on any other occasion. Not one third of those
who presented themselves at the Opera-house were able

to obtain admission. "Caps were lost, and gowns torn to pieces, without number or mercy, in the struggle to get in. Ladies in full dress, who had sent away their carriages, were obliged to appear in the streets and walk home without caps or attendants." "Luckily the weather was fine," adds the Doctor, who witnessed this uncommon spectacle. "The Paganini" thus anticipated the extraordinary triumphs of the more famous artist of half a century later. Signor Paganini, the husband, was only "a coarse first man," and sang almost without a voice. Next comes Ercole Paganini, born at Ferrara, about 1770, the composer of several operas, produced at La Scala, Milan, and at Florence, from 1804 to 1810. A tenor singer named Paganini appeared in opera at Florence in 1830, was decidedly successful and became highly popular in Genoa in 1836. After Francesco Lamperti was appointed (in 1850) professor of singing at the Conservatorio, Milan, among the good pupils he turned out was one named Paganini, of whom, however, no particulars are forthcoming. In 1865, Cesare Paganini, a theoretical writer, published a treatise at Florence; and in November, 1898, Signora Franceschati-Paganini was the Brünnhilde in a performance of "Götterdämmerung," at Bologna. Then there was Dr. Paganini, who was perhaps the brother in whose charge young Nicolo was allowed to go to Lucca in 1798. Whomsoever he may have been, this Dr. Paganini died in 1835, which event gave rise to a rumour that the great violinist was dead — a rumour happily untrue. This Dr. Paganini was not a fiddle-player, but a fiddle-fancier.

He possessed a violin ornamented with mother-o'-pearl
and ebony, which had belonged to a Shah of Persia, the
favourite violin of Lord Byron (so it was said), one that
had belonged to Stanislaus of Poland, father-in-law of
Louis XV., one that had been played upon by Charles IV.
of Spain (the enthusiast who had quartet performances
at six in the morning, and who scorned to " keep
time,") and another, once the property of that monarch's
favourite, Don Manuel de Godoy, Duke of Alcudia.

All the Paganinis mentioned above were eclipsed by *the*
Paganini (*pace* Dr. Burney), the artist who stood alone,
whose life was full of strange vicissitudes, who was
worshipped and calumniated, who was applauded as
perhaps never artist was before nor since, yet who was
laughed at, hissed—only once—brought before the law-
courts — threatened with imprisonment and mobbed
within an ace of being lynched.   As a child of four,
Paganini narrowly escaped being buried alive; from
youth up he was a constant sufferer from physical dis-
orders ; he had no real home till he was fifty-two; after
death his remains were refused burial for five years; and
when his body had rested in the grave for half a century
it was exhumed, apparently in order that his features
might once more be gazed upon.   Truly, Paganini's story
is a romance, a drama, a tragedy.   We may not look
upon his like again, nor is it desirable that we should ;
for his life conveys a moral that few can fail to discern.

The artist is the child of his age.   What kind of age
was it that produced Paganini ?   A few years before he
was born there came into the world one who was to set

Plate II.—See Appendix.

THE BIRTHPLACE OF PAGANINI.

Europe aflame. The age was the age of revolution. Thrones tottered; armies devastated the Continent, and Italy became a mere appanage of the French Empire. The political upheaval was accompanied by a revolution in art. The romantic school in music arose, and Beethoven, Schubert, Berlioz, Chopin, Schumann, Liszt, and Wagner, were the psychic results of the turmoil into which the world was thrown. Into such a world, already feeling the premonitory tremors of the great Revolution, was Nicolo Paganini born, at Genoa, on October 27th, 1782.*

The Genoese—thrifty and industrious—bore no very good moral character at that time; but they were then perhaps not alone in that respect. Little information is available concerning the family of Paganini. The father, Antonio Paganini, kept a small shop in the vicinity of the port; he is described as a man of extraordinarily avaricious character, hard and brutal, but possessing the redeeming quality of a love for music, and showing some skill in the art; his instrument was the mandoline, though Laphaléque says he was a violinist. The mother must have been of a lovable disposition, from what little has been recorded of her. The family consisted of two sons and two daughters. Of the elder son, mention is made but once; of the daughters, nothing seems to be known. Little Nicolo must have given

---

* All biographical notices of Paganini, with the exception of that in Riemann's "Dictionary of Music," give February 18th, 1784, as the date of birth. The correct date seems to have been established when the centenary celebration took place, in 1882.

evidence of musical talent very early, but ere he was put
to his studies he was attacked by the measles, and that so
severely that he remained for a whole day in a state of
catalepsy. He was given up for dead and was wrapped
in a shroud, and only a slight movement at the last,
showing symptoms of life, saved him from the horror of
premature burial. Scarcely had he recovered, when his
father began his lessons in violin playing. The child's
evident disposition for the art excited the father's avarice,
which found little scope for gratification in his small
business undertakings. He indulged in golden dreams
of the future, and to hasten their realisation was un-
remitting in his work of instruction. His method was
cruel in the extreme. The poor child was kept to his
task from morn till night; slight faults were punished
with rigour, even blows and starvation being resorted to
in order to force the talent which nature had bestowed.
This unnatural treatment must have wrung the heart of
the gentle mother, and doubtless by way of encouragement she told the poor little fellow of her wonderful
dream. An Angel had appeared to her, and promised
her the fulfilment of any desire. She asked that her son
might become the greatest of violinists, and her prayer
was to be granted. This disclosure may have fired the
ambition of the child, for he was the hardest of workers,
and needed no spur. Already, at six years of age, he
was a tolerable player, and was even beginning to find
out new paths. His performances excited the admiration and amazement of the neighbours, and even the
Maestro Francesco Gnecco visited the little house by the

harbour to listen to the wonder-child. He introduced
the boy to the circle of his own friends, and made the
father understand that he had long outgrown his training.
In short, the germ of the *virtuoso* of later days was
already manifesting itself. Nicolo was now placed
under Giovanni Servetto, leader of the theatre band—a
man of slight attainments, with whom the boy did not
stay long. His next master was Giacomo Costa, the
foremost violinist in Genoa and maestro di capella of the
Cathedral, a genial man, who took a lively interest in
the boy. Under Costa, Nicolo made rapid progress, and
was introduced to a new world, though the pedantry of
the master frequently came into collision with the pecu-
liarities of the pupil. Young Paganini now had to play
a new concerto each week at one of the churches: that
was one of the conditions Costa imposed when taking
him as a pupil. Paganini's extraordinary powers as a
player at sight were in great measure due to this early
experience. The father still exercised stern oversight,
and there was little relaxation or youthful pleasure for
Nicolo. His health was already undermined, and, as
Dubourg touchingly puts it:—"the sickly child, incap-
able of attaining a healthy maturity, was merged into the
suffering man."

In his eighth year Nicolo composed a sonata for the
violin—since, with other works, lost. About that time a
very vivid, almost shamefaced, impression was made
upon him by hearing that Mozart, at the age of six, had
composed a pianoforte concerto, with parts for orchestra,
and so difficult that only a *virtuoso* could execute it. For

long Nicolo tormented himself with the thought of this
musical superiority, and strove day and night to remedy
his own imperfection in the art.

CHAPTER II.

IN 1793 Paganini made his *début* in the great Theatre of Genoa (the Carlo Felice?). He was in his eleventh year, and his reputation must have been considerable, for the occasion was of some importance, being the benefit concert of two singers of repute, Luigi Marchesi and Teresa Bertinotti.* Marchesi was second only to Pacchierotti among the male *soprani* of the time, and sang at the King's Theatre, London, during the season of 1788; in the " Musical Reminiscences " of the Earl of Mount Edgcumbe he is highly praised as the most brilliant singer of his day. It was a great compliment to the talent of the young Nicolo that these singers should apply for his assistance. Moreover, they promised to sing for him when he should give a concert. Both functions duly took place, and the boy-artist at each played a set of variations of his own composition on " La Carmagnole "; an air then greatly in vogue. That old melody " Malbrough s'en-va-t-en guerre,"

* Anders, and others after him, give the name of the second singer as Albertinotti. No such name can be traced, and it is probable that it was the young Bertinotti, who was a juvenile prodigy, appearing in opera at the age of twelve. She sang in London about the year 1812.

pressed into the service of the French Revolution, was appropriately associated with the young artist, himself a revolutionist. His success was phenomenal, performers and audience being thrown into transports of admiration.

It would appear that young Paganini studied with Giacomo Costa for a period of six months only. He must then have continued to work by himself, for it was not until about 1795 that his father took him to Parma, to place him under the " Pride of Italy," Alessandro Rolla, to whom the boy had been recommended by Costa. There was an affecting farewell between Nicolo and his mother, for they were tenderly attached to each other. Paganini has himself related the story of his interview with Rolla, which, for the sake of completeness, must be summarised here.

When Nicolo with his father arrived at Rolla's house, the famous violinist was ill in bed. His wife showed the visitors into an apartment adjoining, and went to inform her husband of their arrival, but he was disinclined to receive the strangers. On a table in the room where they were waiting lay a violin, and a composition in manuscript—Rolla's latest concerto. Paganini, prompted by his father, took up the violin, and played the concerto through. Astonished at the performance, Rolla asked what *virtuoso* was in the next room, and on being told it was only a boy he had heard, would not credit the statement without the evidence of his own eyes. To the father's entreaty Rolla replied that he could teach the boy nothing; it would waste his time.

to remain with him. He must go to Ferdinando Paer,
who would teach him composition.

There are several versions of this story, and much
uncertainty respecting some points. Rolla was chamber
virtuoso, and director of the concerts at the Court of
Parma. Paer, whose first opera was produced in 1789,
was at this time in great request at Venice, where he
brought out a succession of operas. In 1796 he may
have been in Parma, for his "Griselda" was produced
there that year. Paganini, at some time or other, doubtless did profit by Paer's friendly assistance; but his real
teacher was Gasparo Ghiretti, chamber musician to
Prince Ferdinard of Parma, and the master of Paer.
Ghiretti was a violinist, as were nearly all the Italian
composers of that period. Under Ghiretti, Paganini
went through a systematic course of study in counterpoint
and composition, devoting himself to the instrumental
style. He must, about the same time, have received
violin lessons from Rolla, though he afterwards refused
to acknowledge that he had been his pupil. Fétis tells
of discussions between Rolla and Paganini concerning
the innovations the latter was attempting, for he was
always striving after new effects. As he could but
imperfectly execute what he aimed at, these eccentric
flights did not commend themselves to Rolla, whose
taste and style were of a more severe order. Of Paganini's work in composition little appears to be known.
Anders states that Paer when in Parma devoted several
hours daily to Paganini; and at the end of the fourth
month entrusted him with a composition of a *duo*, in which

Nicolo succeeded to the complete satisfaction of his master. Paganini may also at that time have sketched, if he did not complete, the Studies, or Caprices, Op. 1.

In 1797 the father took the boy from Parma, and set out with him on a tour through Lombardy. Concerts were given in Milan, Bologna, Florence, Pisa, and Leghorn.

The young artist achieved an extraordinary reputation ; the father took possession of the more material rewards of art. The "golden dreams" were in process of realisation! Returning to Genoa, young Paganini finished the composition of his Twenty-four Studies, which were of such excessive difficulty that he could not play them. He would try a single passage over in a hundred ways, working for ten or eleven hours at a stretch, and then would come the inevitable collapse. He was still under the stern domination of his father, and his spirit must have chafed under the bondage. His own ardour was sufficient to carry his labours to the verge of exhaustion, and he needed no spur as an incentive to exertion. In all directions save that of music his education was utterly neglected. The moral side of his nature was allowed to grow wild. There was the restraining influence of a mother's love, but there was little else. It might indeed be said that, musically, Paganini was self-educated; but that one of the world's great geniuses should lack the intellectual and moral training that go to make the complete man was sad in the extreme. Paganini's was a nature warped; on the one side phenomenal power, on the other bodily suffering, intellectual and spiritual atrophy. But more of this when we turn from his career to the man himself.

As the youth grew older the spirit of revolt arose. He must and would escape from the tryanny of his avaricious father. But how? A way soon offered itself. At Lucca, the festival of St. Martin, held each November, was an event of such importance, musically, that it drew visitors from all parts of Italy. As the November of 1798 drew near, young Paganini besought his father's permission to attend the festival, but his request was met by a point-blank refusal. The importunities of the youth, aided by the prayers of the mother, at length prevailed, and in care of the elder brother afterwards Dr. Paganini (?)—Nicolo was allowed to leave home.

Free at last, the youth, now in his seventeenth year, went on his way, his whole being thrilled with dreams of success and happiness. At Lucca he was most enthusiastically received, and, elated by his good fortune, Paganini extended his tour, playing in Pisa and other towns. Enabled now to earn his own living, Paganini determined never to return to the home where he had suffered so much. His father must have obtained information as to the youth's whereabouts, for it has been stated that he managed to obtain a large part of the young artist's earnings. The money was freely yielded to a certain extent, and the residue was obtained by threats. But no threat or entreaty could induce Nicolo to return to his paternal home. The bird had escaped, and liberty was sweet. But young Paganini was scarcely fitted for an independent, uncontrolled career. He had no moral ballast, and much would depend upon what kind of company he kept.

One has to bear in mind that at the period now under notice—1798—Europe was in a very unsettled state. The very pillars of society were shaken, and there were many dangers in the path of the young and inexperienced. But that is a very trite observation, for it applies to all times and places. However, Paganini seems to have become acquainted with what Fétis terms "artists of another kind," who encouraged "play" of a more exciting, if less exalted order, than the young musician had hitherto devoted himself to. With his ardent southern temperament Paganini threw himself with the greatest zest into the vortex of gambling, and frequently lost at a sitting the earnings of several concerts and was reduced to the greatest embarrassment. Soon his talent provided fresh resources, and his days ran on in alternations of good and evil fortune. Tall, slight, delicate and handsome,* Paganini, despite his frail constitution, was an object of attraction to the fair sex. Incidents in his early manhood probably formed the foundation for some of the stories told of him later, As Fétis puts it ; the enthusiasm for art, love and "play," reigned by turns in his soul. He ought to have been careful of himself, but he went to excess in everything. Then came a period of enforced repose, of absolute exhaustion, lasting sometimes for weeks. . This would be followed by a display

---

* William Gardiner many years later spoke of the transparent delicacy of Paganini's complexion, and said of his little son Achille that he was the handsomest boy he had ever seen.

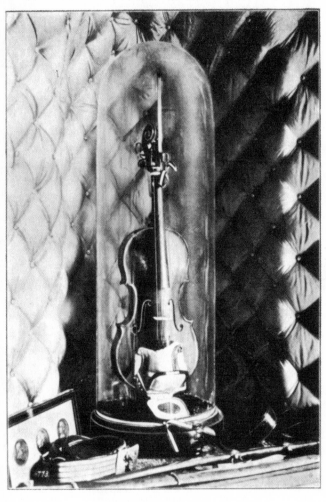

Plate III.—See Appendix.

PAGANINI'S VIOLIN IN THE MUNICIPAL MUSEUM
AT GENOA.

of extraordinary energy, when his marvellous talent took its highest flights, and he plunged once more into the wildest bohemianism. Such a course of life was enough to wreck the artist, and no friend seemed to be at hand to save him from himself. Frequently he had to part with his violin in order to raise money to pay his debts of honour, and it was upon one such occasion that he met with the greatest good fortune he had yet experienced, and acquired a violin which became the instrument of his conversion from the fatal passion for gambling.

Arriving at Leghorn, where he was to give a concert, Paganini yielded to his weakness for the other kind of play and lost his money and his violin. He was in a dilemma indeed, but was fortunate in meeting with an enthusiastic musical amateur, M. Livron, a French merchant, the owner of a superb Guarnerius violin. This instrument M. Livron lent to the young artist, and attended the concert. When Paganini went to return the violin to its owner, M. Livron at once exclaimed, " I shall take care never to profane the strings your fingers have touched. It is to you now that my violin belongs." A noble benefactor, that M. Livron. The Guarnerius became Paganini's inseparable companion ; he played upon it throughout all his tours, and its subsequent history will be duly related.

Paganini acquired another instrument on the same easy terms, but attended by different circumstances. Signor Pasini, of Parma, a painter of some distinction, and an amateur violinist, had heard of Paganini's wonderful powers as a reader of music at sight, but refused to

credit the statements. Pasini one day placed before
Paganini a manuscript concerto, in which difficulties of
all kinds were brought together, and putting into the
artist's hands a splendid Stradivari violin, said: "This
instrument is yours if you can play that at sight, like a
master, without studying its difficulties in advance." "If
that is so," replied Paganini, " You may bid farewell to
it at once." His terrific* execution made the music
seem as if it played itself as his eye fell upon it. Pasini
was petrified with astonishment.

The abandonment of the vice of gambling came about
in this way, his own words being quoted. " I shall never
forget," said he, "one day placing myself in a position
which was to decide my whole career. The Prince
De * * * * * had long desired to possess my excellent
violin (the Guarnerius), the only one I then had, and
which I still possess. One day he desired me to fix a
price ; but, unwilling to part from my instrument, I
declared I would not sell it for less than 250 gold
Napoleons. A short time after, the Prince remarked
that I was probably indulging in banter in asking so
high a price, and added that he was disposed to give
2,000 francs for it. Precisely that very day I found
myself in great want of money, in consequence of a
heavy loss at play, and I almost resolved to yield my
violin for the sum he had offered, when a friend came in
to invite me to a party that evening. My capital then
consisted of thirty francs, and I had already deprived

---

* Fétis calls it "Foudroyante exécution."

myself of my jewels, watch, rings, pins, etc. I instantly formed the resolve to risk this last resource, and if fortune went against me, to sell the violin and to set out for St. Petersburg, without instrument and without funds, with the object of retrieving my position. Soon my thirty francs were reduced to three, and I saw myself on the road to the great city, when fortune, changing in the twinkling of an eye, gained me one hundred francs with the little that yet remained. That moment saved my violin and set me up again. From that day I withdrew from play, to which I had sacrificed a portion of my youth : and convinced that a gambler is universally despised, I renounced for ever that fatal passion."

It would be interesting to know when these things occurred, but dates are wanting ; it is sufficient to find the artist triumphant in one great crisis in his life. Gambling, to which, however, he was not a party, was destined to trouble the last years of his life, as will be seen further on.

Paganini's career, gambling apart, was by no means of a conventional character. His irregular habits, fits of extraordinary energy followed by langour and depression, led to frequent disappearances from public view. One such disappearance lasted for about four years, and only the romantic aspect of it has been described ; the prime cause may have been overlooked. Here is one view of the matter. Enter Napoleon ; exit Paganini. In 1800 Napoleon crossed the Alps ; in 1804, he proclaimed himself Emperor. He parcelled out Europe, providing for his brothers and sisters, creating sovereigns at his own sweet will. Italy, invaded by a foreign foe, shaken with wars, "alarums and excursions," was not a happy hunting ground for a travelling virtuoso. Paganini vanished from view. In absolute retirement he lived for over three years at the chateau of a Tuscan lady of rank, who was a performer upon the guitar. Paganini threw himself with ardour into the study of that instrument, and became as great a virtuoso upon it as upon the violin. He composed a number of pieces for guitar and violin. According to Fétis, Paganini also devoted himself to the study of agriculture.

But eventually he tired of a life of indolence and dalliance, and in 1804—the country settled now under French government—Paganini returned to Genoa, but whether to the paternal roof is not clear. He was doubtless invigorated by his long rest, and now resumed his arduous course of study. It has been remarked that it was only after Paganini had attained an almost perfect mastery over his instrument that he began to investigate the methods of other virtuosi*; even so, he had formed his own style of composition before studying the works of others. Now, he busied himself with the studies of Locatelli, whose extravagances almost equalled his own. It is said that he even gave lessons while in Genoa, and mention is made of one pupil, Catarina Calcagno, who had a brilliant, but brief career.

In 1805, Paganini resumed his artistic tours, and arriving at Lucca, played a concerto at an evening festival in a convent church. So great was the enthusiasm of the

---

* Naumann, "History of Music," p. 1140 (English Edition.)

audience (or congregation), that the monks had to leave their stalls to put a stop to the applause.   At that time, Maria Anna (Elise), sister of Napoleon, was Princess of Lucca, and the Tuscan court was held in that Capital. The fame of Paganini could not fail to have reached the ears of the Princess, and it was but natural that the first *virtuoso* of Italy should receive an official appointment. So it happened that in the year 1805 he was offered, and accepted, the post of leader of the Court orchestra, and solo violinist.   He also gave violin lessons to Prince Bacciochi, the husband of Maria Anna.   It was during this period that Paganini began his experiments of employing less than the four strings of his violin.   He gave an account of the origin of the practice to a friend at Prague many years later.*   " It fell to my lot," he said, " to direct the opera whenever the reigning family visited it, as well as to perform at Court three times a week, and to get up a public concert for the higher circles every fortnight.   Whenever these were visited by the Princess, she never remained to the close, because the flageolet tones of my violin were too much for her nerves.   On the other hand there was another fascinating creature. . . . . . . who, I flattered myself, felt a penchant for me, and was never absent from my performances ; on my own side, I had long been her admirer (Paganini was now twenty-three years of age, susceptible, and possibly himself fascinating.) Our mutual fondness became gradually stronger and stronger ; but we were forced to conceal it, and by this means its strength and fervour were sensibly enhanced.

---

* Professor Julius Schottky.

One day I promised to surprise her at the next concert,
with a musical joke, which should convey an allusion to
our attachment; and I accordingly gave notice at Court
that I should bring forward a musical novelty, under the
title of 'A Love Scene.' The whole world was on tiptoe
at the tidings; and on the evening appointed, I made my
appearance, violin in hand; I had previously robbed it of
the two middle strings, so that none but E and G remained.
The first string being designed to play the maiden's part,
and the second (fourth) the youth's, I began with a species
of dialogue, in which I attempted to introduce movements
analogous to transient bickerings and reconciliations
between the lovers. Now my strings growled, and then
sighed; and anon they lisped, hesitated, joked and joyed,
till at last they sported with merry jubilee. In the course
of time, both souls joined once more in harmony, and the
appeased lovers' quarrel led to a *pas de deux*, which ter-
minated in a brilliant *coda*. This musical fantasia of mine
was greeted with loud applause. The lady, to whom every
scene referred, rewarded me by looks full of delight and
sweetness, and the Princess was charmed into such amiable condescension, that she loaded me with encomiums
—asking me, whether, since I could produce so much with
two strings, it would not be possible for me to gratify them
by playing on *one*. I yielded instant assent—the idea
tickled my fancy—and, as the Emperor's birthday occurred
some weeks afterwards (August 15th,) I composed a sonata
for the G string, which I entitled ' Napoleon,' and played
before the Court to so much effect, that a cantata, by
Cimarosa, given the same evening, fell through without

Plate IV.—See Appendix.

CARICATURE PUBLISHED 1831.

producing any impression on its hearers.* This is the genuine and original cause of my prejudice in favour for the G string. People were afterwards importunate to hear more of this performance, and in this way I became day by day a greater adept at it, and acquired constantly increasing confidence in this peculiar mystery of handling the bow." More of the " Napoleon Sonata " later.

When the Princess became Grand Duchess of Tuscany, the Court removed to Florence, and Paganini, as a matter of course, was in the retinue. His official career, however, came to an abrupt termination in the early part of 1813. When appointed Court Musical Director, Paganini was accorded the rank of Captain in the Royal Guard, and, as such, was permitted to wear a brilliant uniform, Appearing in this garb at a State function at Florence, in 1813, the artist was " commanded " to change it for the ordinary dress suit. This request Paganini construed as an insult, and refused compliance ; whereupon there was a sudden rupture, and instant resignation of office. Paganini, at different times, obtained leave of absence, and undertook various professional tours ; and as he met with some strange experiences, we will follow him in his wanderings.

---

* Cimarosa, who died in 1801, espoused the revolutionary cause when the French army entered Italy, and was imprisoned and condemned to death when the reaction came, but was restored to liberty on condition of leaving Naples. He would, naturally, have been popular with the Bonapartists, and it was rather ungenerous vanity on the part of Paganini to have exulted over this particular success.

CHAPTER III.

IN 1808 occurred the first of these excursions. Paganini went to Leghorn, the scene of his early triumphs.
He had not been there for seven years, but his first
concert, this visit, was attended with some unpleasant mis-
haps. He had run a nail into his heel, and came limping
on the stage, whereupon the audience set up a titter—an
incident quite enough to upset a sensitive artist. Then,
just as he was commencing his concerto, the candles fell
from his music-stand, and the laughter was unrestrained;
after a few bars of his solo, the first string of his violin
snapped, and the merriment became uproarious ; but he
finished the performance upon the three strings, and the
artist soon converted the audience to a demonstration of
a more grateful character. Thus his "one string" experience served him in good stead.

At Ferrara something worse befell. For his concert
there, Paganini had engaged a vocalist, Signora Marietta
Marcolini ; but at the last moment, the lady, either from
indisposition or caprice, refused to sing. Paganini went
to his hostel boiling with rage, but was somewhat mollified
on being told there was a lady occupying an apartment
in the same house, who might perhaps take the place of

the recalcitrant singer. This was Signora Pallerini, the
principal dancer at the theatre, who had a very agreeable
voice, but who made no pretension to being a singer,
although she was not without training and talent. Paganini lost no time in seeking the young dancer, and by dint
of perseverance obtained her consent to his wish.

But when the Signora came on to sing she was seized
with stage-fright. Her voice failed her, and her song
produced no effect. Paganini offered his arm to conduct
her behind the scenes, but just before they reached the
wing, a shrill whistle was heard—equivalent to a hiss in
England. This was too much; the poor *débutante* lost
consciousness, and fell into the arms of her friend. Pale
with rage, Paganini promised himself a signal vengeance.
The concert was drawing to a close when the angry artist
whispered to Signora Pallerini, "Come! Listen!" He
rushed on the stage, and announcing to the audience that
he would conclude the concert with a musical jest, proceeded to imitate the cries of various animals, the chirping
of birds, the howling of dogs, and the crowing of cocks;
then, with a stolen glance towards the wing, as if to make
known the carrying out of his revenge, he advanced to
the footlights, rested his bow on the "chanterelle," close
to the bridge, and with a single stroke brought it violently
on the "G," producing distinctly the sound of the donkey's
hee-haw! "This is for the man who whistled," he exclaimed,
with an air of triumph, and for the second time gave his
imitation—with added energy. Then he awaited the shouts
of laughter that should assail the poor whistler, but something quite different happened. The pit rose to a man,

and howling, whistling, and stamping, the audience proceeded to storm the stage ; and only precipitate flight by
means of a private door, saved the unlucky artist's life.
The explanation came to Paganini later. The inhabit-
ants of the villages around Ferrara had from time imme-
morial a strong prejudice against their Capital. The citizens they alleged were stupid in their nature, and deserved
the sobriquet " hee-haw." If a countryman, returning
from Ferrara, were asked where he came from, he replied
by throwing back his head and braying like an ass! Paganini had no knowledge of local history ; he was not a reader,
he never even glanced at the papers, except when they
contained something concerning himself. His revenge
caused quite a tumult, in what way can be well perceived :
and the magistrate, to restore quiet, advised Paganini
not to give his second concert in the town, so that the
offenders were really punished all round.

It is not necessary to enter into details concerning all
Paganini's tours. It appears to have been in 1810 that
he wrote the " Napoleon Sonata," and he performed it in
public at a concert given by him at Parma, August 18th,
1811. His fame was spreading beyond his own country,
and Schilling states that from 1812 the German musical
journals bestowed much attention upon him. He was at
Milan in 1813, and his success there was greater than
ever. For that city he appeared to have a predilection,
for he was there, with the exception of a short stay at
Genoa, until the autumn of 1814. At that time he was
by no means a recluse. He visited the theatre, La Scala,
and witnessed a performance of Vigano's ballet, " Il Noce

di Benevento," to which Süssmayer wrote the music; and from a certain scene he took the theme of his variations known as " Le Streghe." At a theatre he was inspired to write one of his finest movements. He went to hear Demarini, Italy's greatest tragedian, and was so affected by one scene that he could not sleep, and his emotion ultimately found expression in music. This will be dealt with when noticing his compositions.

In October, 1814, Paganini went to Bologna, and there met Rossini for the first time. Rossini, nine years the junior of Paganini, had already produced a dozen operas— two in Milan that year. By Court favour Rossini had just escaped the conscription, and had hastened away to Bologna. The meeting of these artists was of importance to both. Meyerbeer went to Italy in 1815, and was there for some years, producing several operas. Laphaléque tells a story to this effect : Meyerbeer was on the eve of leaving Florence to proceed to Naples to bring out one of his works. He did not yet know that place, and it offered a double attraction; he wanted to enjoy the beautiful blue sky as well as his artistic triumph. But he went to hear Paganini, and dreamt no more of Naples, nor of his opera. Paganini travelled all through Tuscany, and Meyerbeer followed ; and not until he had heard Paganini eighteen times could he tear himself away from him.

Within the period of five years, Paganini returned to Milan five times, making a long stay on each occasion, and giving a great number of concerts. He played at Verona, Padua—where the " prison " stories seem to have originated—returned to Milan early in 1816, when he met the French violinist, Charles Lafont, with whom he played and of whom more will be said. Then to Venice, Trieste, and back to Venice in time to hear Spohr (October 18th), on whom he called both before and after the concert. Spohr greatly desired to hear Paganini play, but the latter excused himself.

Paganini must ere this have received invitations to visit other countries, for Spohr in his diary remarks, when referring to Paganini's first visit, that he had apparently abandoned his project of going to Vienna. In 1817, Paganini visited Piacenza, where he met the Polish violinist, Karl Joseph von Lipinski, who had gone to Italy expressly to hear Paganini. The Italian treated his Polish brother artist generously, and played with him at two concerts. Paganini was also again at Milan that year and paid a visit to his mother at Genoa. According to Anders, his father died in 1817. At the close of the same year Paganini was in Rome, where Rossini's opera " La Cenerentola " was produced at the opening of the Carnival season, December 26th. It is related that Meyerbeer was also in Rome at this time, and that Rossini's " Carnovale " was sung in the streets by the composer, Meyerbeer, and Paganini, who disguised themselves for the frolic. Paganini, in the Palace of Prince von Kaunitz, the Austrian Ambassador, was introduced to Prince Metternich, who, charmed with his talent, pressed him to visit Vienna. But the violinist's health was in a precarious state. He suffered from an intestinal disorder, aggravated by his addiction to some quack remedy. He gave concerts in Rome, of which Schilling, who gives the date, however,

as 1827, gives a very curious account. The first concert,
though held in a Palace—such buildings being met with at
every step—was in a room like a hay-loft. The orchestra
consisted of some half-dozen shabbily dressed players, the
singers were mechanics, members of the chorus of the
Teatro Argentina, and the audience scarcely numbered
fifty. Rome, professedly the first musical city of Italy,
and of Europe, was ignorant of Paganini, the greatest
violin virtuoso of Italy and the world. But his extraordinary genius kindled coldness into enthusiasm. At his
second concert the attendance increased tenfold ; at the
third the success was even greater.

In 1818, and the following year, he gave concerts at
Verona, Turin, Florence, and other towns. At Verona,
the conductor of the theatre orchestra, one Valdabrini,
persuaded himself that Paganini was little else than a
charlatan, one who might play the pieces of his own
repertory very well, but who could not execute a work
such as a concerto of his, Valdabrini's, composition.
Paganini was informed of this estimate of his abilities,
and hastened to assure Valdabrini that he would be happy
to reproduce the inspirations of the *chef d'orchestre* of
Verona ; and as this trial would be a powerful attraction,
he would reserve it for his last concert. The day of
rehearsal arrived, and Paganini was in his place. Instead
of the music of the concerto, however, the artist improvised all kinds of fanciful passages, insomuch that the
astonished orchestral players, lost in admiration, forgot
to go on with their own work, The disappointed Valdabrini exclaimed : " My friend, this is not my concerto

you are playing, I can recognise nothing of what I have written." " Don't distress yourself," replied Paganini, " at the concert you will recognise your work well enough, only now I claim a little indulgence."

The concert night arrived, and Paganini commenced with pieces of his own choice, reserving the concerto for the end. All were attention for the great event. Paganini came on at last, holding in his hand a Malacca walking cane. Everyone asked himself : What will he do with that ? Suddenly he seized his violin, and, employing the cane as a bow, played the concerto (thought by the composer to be practicable only after long study) from beginning to end, not only rendering the most difficult passages, but introducing charming variations, never failing for an instant to display the purity, grace and verve that characterised his art.* This pleasantry was not to the taste of Valdabrini, we may be sure ; but it was a rebuke to his presumption. Such amenities are scarcely possible now-a-days.

Paganini visited Naples in 1819 for the first time. When he arrived he found the local musicians badly disposed towards him, and he had something like a repetition of his experience at Verona, only he used the cane no more ! These musicians affected to doubt the reality of the marvels fame attributed to Paganini, and proposed to amuse themselves at his expense. They engaged a young composer, Danna (Dana ?)† fresh from the Conservatorio, to write a string quartet, filled with difficulties

---

* Laphaléque.

† Son of Giuseppe Dana, of Naples?

of every kind—for the first violin—persuading themselves
that the great violinist could not overcome them. When
all was ready—no doubt the other parts had been well
practised—Paganini was invited to a musical réunion,
where he found the violinists Onorio de Vito, Giuseppe
Mario Festa, the violoncellist Ciandelli, and the composer Danna. Hardly had he arrived, when they placed
the music before him, and invited him to play it at sight.
Perceiving that they had set a trap for him, Paganini
cast a hurried glance at the music, and played it off as
though it had long been familiar to him. Confounded
by what they heard, his assistants were prodigal in their
admiration, and declared him incomparable.

Paganini's health now gave way to an alarming degree,
and his landlord, fearing the malady was consumption—
infectious, according to current opinion—proceeded to turn
the violinist and his belongings into the street. Medical
science has confirmed the views of the Neapolitans in
respect to the contagious character of consumption, and the
open-air treatment is now considered the proper method
to adopt ; but the landlord's rough and ready application
of the remedy was highly objectionable, and so thought
Ciandelli, who chanced to be passing at the time. He
gave the landlord a severe thrashing, and conveyed Paganini to more comfortable lodgings, where he was carefully
tended. Paganini repaid this act of kindness, as will be
seen. These little scenes throw curious side-lights on life
in Naples at that period.

In 1820, Paganini returned to Milan, where he founded
an Amateur Society, *Gli Orfei*, and conducted its concerts

for a time ; but the roving habits he had acquired rendered
a settled life irksome, and he was soon again on the move.
The winter found him once more in Rome, where he
must have stayed on and off for another year ; for he was
there in December, 1821, when Rossini was about to
produce his opera, " Matilda di Sabran," at the opening
of the Carnival season. On the day of the last rehearsal
the conductor fell ill, and Rossini was in despair to replace
him. Paganini, hearing of his friend's dilemma, offered
to conduct the rehearsal and the first performance—his
operatic experience at Lucca must not be forgotten—an
offer Rossini gratefully accepted. Without a moment's
preparation, Paganini set to work to communicate to an
unskilled orchestra—it was at the *Teatro d'Apollone*—the
composer's intentions and the manner in which they
should be interpreted. Having no time for verbal explanation, he did everything by example, playing the first violin
part an octave higher than it was written, and making
himself heard above the strongest *fortissimo*. At a glance
he penetrated the meaning of every movement, and he so
worked upon the executants that they obeyed him as if
by enchantment. This single rehearsal sufficed to bring
about an irreproachable performance, the orchestra
undergoing a veritable metamorphosis, to the astonishment of everyone, Rossini included. So far Laphaléque.
Sutherland Edwards* says Paganini conducted the first
three performances, adding, " Never, it is said, did the
band of the ' Apollo ' play with so much spirit before."

For the next two years Paganini was constantly travel-

---

* The Life of Rossini, p. 226.

ling, and in the year 1823 we have the first glimpse of him through the medium of an English musical journal.* This first reference is quite incidental. Giuseppe Rastrelli was playing in Naples in 1822 (or 1823), and was well received, "although his predecessor, the celebrated Paganini," was still fresh in the public remembrance. This assumes that Paganini was well known to English readers. He had indeed been mentioned in books published before this date. On his way to Pavia in 1823, Paganini was attacked with illness, and his life was despaired of. At that time he had again intended going to Austria, but a long rest was needed to restore his health. This repose he enjoyed at Genoa, and recovered sufficiently to give two concerts in the *Teatro da Sant' Agostino*, in 1824. The second concert introduced two youthful claimants to public favour. The first was a Signora Bianchi, under twenty years of age, who was characterised in the bills as the little *virtuosa forestiera*, and who sang three airs ; the other was a Signora Barette, who played a *Pezzo Cantabile* and a *Sonatina* upon the violoncello. They both experienced a flattering reception.† The young violoncellist was not more than fourteen years old, and there is no reason to suppose that she was the first of her sex to appear in public as a violon-

---

* With the exception of a Literary Supplement to the "New Musical and Universal Magazine," 1774, there was no publication devoted to Music until the year 1818, when "The Quarterly Musical Magazine and Review" appeared, edited by Robert Mackenzie Bacon. This was followed in 1823 by "The Harmonicon," edited by William Ayrton.

† Harmonicon, Vol. III., p. 37.

cellist. The other "little guest" or stranger was to play an important part in Paganini's history.

This concert afforded another proof of Paganini's power of attraction. A certain M. Bergman, a (Swedish?) traveller and passionate lover of music, reading accidentally the evening before in the journal at Leghorn, an announcement of Paganini's concert, lost no time, but instantly set out for Genoa, a distance of a hundred miles, and luckily reached the spot just half an hour before the concert began. He went with his expectations raised to the utmost, but, to use his own expression, the reality was as far above his anticipations as the heavens are above the earth. Nor could this enthusiastic amateur rest content with once hearing Paganini, but actually followed him to Milan, in order to hear him exercise his talents a second time. Now-a-days the enthusiasts are young ladies, who mob their favourites in the artists' room!

In 1824 Paganini gave two concerts in *La Scala*, Milan, which was crowded to excess. At the first he played a concerto, and three airs with variations—all on the fourth string, so said the report. A surfeit, this, even for his fervent admirers. In the same year at Pavia, he gave two concerts, the bills being headed:

PAGANINI
Farà sentire il suo Violino.

(Paganini will cause his violin to be heard.) He was received with no less enthusiasm than at Milan. Paganini then returned to Genoa, but soon left for Venice.

There he formed an union with Antonia Bianchi, the young singer he introduced at Genoa, who became his companion, sang at his concerts, and shared his triumphs.

In 1825, Paganini was again at Naples, where he gave a concert, causing his name to be announced in the bills as—

Filarmonico,

a term which gave rise to much discussion, some considering it as indicating modesty, others just the reverse; but at all events it savoured of affectation. In the summer of 1825, Paganini went to Palermo, where he also gave a concert. The delicious climate of Sicily had a great charm for him, and he remained there for nearly a year, giving concerts at different places, but enjoying prolonged intervals of repose. His health strengthened, Paganini again entertained the idea of leaving Italy, but determined upon one more tour before carrying out his intention. In 1826, he visited Trieste, Venice, and finally Rome, where he gave five concerts. In April, 1827, Pope Leo XII. invested Paganini with the order of the Golden Spur, a distinction so rare that it afforded a topic for conversation for some time. From Rome Paganini went to Florence, and as " Il Cavaliere Paganini " gave a concert at the *Teatro Pergola*, which was attended by all the rank and fashion of the place. He was detained for some time at Florence owing to a disease breaking out in one of his legs. As soon as he was able to travel he set out for Milan, where he was received with every demonstration of affection. He gave four musical soirées at the close of 1827, and in the early part of 1828, two concerts in *La Scala*, when he appears to have played for the first time the concerto with the " Rondo ad un Campanello ; " the piece created a great effect. Paganini had now traversed the whole of Italy at least three times, giving hundreds of concerts, building up an ever growing reputation and exciting universal admiration, despite those detractors whose machinations have been exposed. At last, on the 2nd of March, 1828, Paganini started on his long projected visit to Vienna.

CHAPTER IV.

PAGANINI arrived at Vienna, March 16th, 1828, and gave his first concert in the Redouten-Saal* on the 29th of the same month, creating a *furore* the like of which had never been witnessed. It must be borne in mind that Paganini was now no romantic-looking youth to move the feelings of sentimental or hysterical young ladies. He was in his forty-sixth year, and his face bore the marks of suffering; he wore his long hair in ringlets falling over his shoulders, but physically he was a wreck. Yet no youthful artist of to-day has made a more sensational *début* than that of Paganini in the Austrian Capital in 1828. To repeat the oft-quoted account given by Schilling: "At the first stroke of the bow on his Guarnerius, one might almost say at the first step he took into the hall, his reputation was decided in Germany. Kindled as by an electric flash, he suddenly shone and sparkled like a miraculous apparition in the domain of art."

Another account, if less familiar, is equally interesting. In a letter from Vienna, addressed to the *Literary Gazette*, the writer says:—" The great novelty and prodigy of the

* Where Beethoven gave his concerts in 1814.

day is one M. Paganini, an Italian peformer on the violin.

"This is the first time he has left Italy; but I heard him previously, about five years ago, at Milan, in competition with M. Lafont, whom he beat fairly.* He is, without contradiction, not only the finest player on the violin, but no other performer, upon what instrument soever, can be styled his equal: Kalkbrenner, Rode, Romberg, Moscheles, Jew and Gentile, are his inferiors by at least some thousand degrees; they are not fit, as we say in Germany, to *reach him water*. He is Mathews of the violin, performs a whole concert on a single string, where you are sure to hear, besides his own instrument, a harp, a guitar, and a flute. In one word, he is a necromancer, and bids fair to beat *la Giraffe*. We have here hats, shawls, gloves and nonsense of every description, *à la Giraffe ;* but yesterday I actually ate *Auflaufy*—a very innocent, rather insipid sweetmeat—*à la Paganini* . . . He has already performed twice to crowded houses in our great masquerade-hall. The beginning of the concert was, as usual, advertised for half-past eleven [in the morning]: at eleven o'clock not a pin dropping from the roof would have reached the ground ; people were already there at nine o'clock. He came hither with six florins in his pocket; now you may style him a warm man. From Vienna he intends to proceed to Paris, and thence to London."†

Here a brief digression is pardonable. The Pasha of

---

* The writer's memory played him false. The meeting with Lafont took place in 1816; or, according to some, in 1812!

† This letter was reproduced in the "Harmonicon."

Egypt, a short time before Paganini's visit, had presented to the Emperor of Austria a Giraffe, an animal then new to Europe. That interesting quadruped, a superb specimen of its kind, created such a sensation, and so completely absorbed public attention, that as seen in the letter just quoted, everything was *à la Giraffe.** Paganini's phenomenal success gained him a popularity that quite eclipsed the poor Giraffe, and now the mode was *à la Paganini*. All kinds of articles were named after him ; a good stroke at billiards was a *coup à la Paganini ;* his bust in butter and crystallised sugar figured on every banquet table ; and portraits, more or less faithful, adorned snuff-boxes, cigar-boxes, or were carved on the canes carried by the fops. Paganini himself went into a shop one day to buy gloves. "*A la Giraffe ?* " asked the salesman. " No, no, some other animal," said the *maestro*, whereupon he was handed a pair *à la Paganini* ! It is said that a certain driver, whom Paganini had once engaged, obtained permission to paint on his vehicle the words *Cabriolet de Paganini*, by which means he gained notoriety and enough money to set up as a hotel-keeper. Paganini was much sought after by the leaders of society and fashion ; but Prince Metternich alone received the favour of a visit.

It may be remembered that Franz Schubert gave his first, and as it turned out, his only concert, in the hall of the Musik-Verein, Vienna, on the 26th of March, three

---

† Lady Morgan, in her book, "France in 1829-30," gives an account of the Giraffe just then arrived in Paris. The animal was added to the collection in the London Zoological Gardens in 1836.

days before that of Paganini.   Schubert cleared over
£30—the first piece of luck that came to the poor composer.   The money flowed freely ; he paid his five Gulden
(something over six shillings) to hear Paganini, and went
a second time, not so much for his own sake, as to take
his friend Bauernfeld,* who had not five farthings, while
with him (Schubert) " money was as plentiful as black-
berries."   Generous, simple Schubert ! Did he and Paganini ever meet ?   What a pair they would have made !

Paganini's Vienna concerts were so successful that
he increased the number from six to twelve.   It it said
that poor musicians actually sold their clothes to raise
the needful in order to hear him ; and that no halls were
large enough to contain all who wished to attend his
concerts.   Paganini's last concert was given by express
command of the Emperor of Austria, who honoured the
occasion by his presence.   Among other things, Paganini introduced the National hymn " God preserve the
Emperor," which he performed with a truth and fervour
of expression that seemed to impart a novelty even to so
familiar a theme.   He did some wonderful things on the
G string, astonishing and delighting all present, especially
rivetting the attention of the Emperor, who led the
applause.

The Court Gazette announced that His Majesty, as a
testimony of his admiration, had sent Paganini a diploma,
appointing him one of the Emperor's chamber musicians,
and exempting him from the usual fees of office ; this
was accompanied by a splendid gold snuff-box set with

---

* A Litterateur, of Vienna ; writer of comedies, etc.

brilliants. The chief magistrate of Vienna presented
Paganini with the gold medal of San Salvador; and, to
crown all, a medal was struck in Paganini's honour.
This, the work of J. Lang, has on the face a portrait in
relief of the violinist, with the inscription:—

NICOLAO PAGANINI Vindobona

MDCCCXXVIII.

and on the back the words:—

Perituris Sonis non Peritura Gloria.

surrounding an open music book with the theme of the
"Bell Rondo," upon which lies the famous Guarnerius
wreathed with laurel. This was the city's parting gift
to the great artist.

These doings were too good to escape the notice of the
caricaturist, and a two-act piece was produced at the
Theater an der Wien, entitled "The Counterfeit Virtuoso;
or, the Concerto on the G string," the music by Kapellmeister Franz Gläser. The overture was ingeniously
made up of the principal subjects of Paganini's concertos,
ludicrously contrasted with counter subjects of a popular
kind. Several of the *quodlibets* were full of humour, and,
with the *bon mots* and anecdotes, tended to make it a
very amusing production for the moment.

It was at Vienna that the rumour spread abroad of
Paganini being in league with the Devil, which accounted
for his marvellous performances. The great violinist
was much disturbed and annoyed by these calumnies,
and had to appeal to the press for aid in refuting them.
It may be that his estrangement from the world, his

love of solitude, morose temper, and the avarice which displayed itself, all had their origin in the hostile attitude assumed by a section of the public during his foreign tours, for when in Italy Paganini seems to have lived much as others did. Paganini was accompanied by his companion Signora Bianchi, and the son born to them, when he visited Vienna.

It was in May the little party left Vienna. The concerts had quite prostrated Paganini, and the family went to Carlsbad. After resting there some time Paganini departed for Prague, but an abscess in the face kept him a prisoner for three weeks. Here is a contemporary account which is interesting. Paganini was obliged to place himself under the care of two celebrated medical men, Krumblholz and Nusshardt, and they were the only visitors he received during his lonely residence up three pair of stairs. After a successful operation on the jaw-bone, one of his physicians expressed a desire which was cherished in vain by the whole city—that of hearing some notes from the hitherto silent instrument of the great master ; and he entreated him to try if he could rest his violin on his hardly healed chin. Paganini confirmed what has long been said, that even before friends he was very niggardly in the display of his talents. He took his instrument, played one stroke with his bow, and said, " *Es geht schon* " (that will do). " For eight days before the first concert," continues the writer, " every place was engaged. When I reached the theatre at four o'clock in the afternoon, it appeared as if the house was about to be stormed, so great was the throng on the outside. Many

Plate V.—See Appendix.

FROM A CONTEMPORARY GERMAN PICTURE.

magistrates and people of the first rank were amongst the crowd, and shared my anxious expection. At last I found myself, I scarcely know how, in the pit, and there awaited for two hours and a half the opening of the concert." The writer then goes on to describe the violinist, his appearance, his smile that made everyone shudder, and the extraordinary performance which roused the audience to the wildest enthusiasm. He then quotes the saying of a Vienna critic : " Paganini has nothing in common with other players but the violin and the bow," and regrets that his friend will not for some time have the opportunity of hearing the superb performer, for he learns that Paganini does not yet intend to visit Paris or London.*

Paganini's first concert only was well attended. There was then a reaction. Some attributed the falling off to the high prices charged for admission, but there was, in fact, a traditional hostility in art matters between Prague and Vienna ; that which was praised in Vienna must be condemned in Prague, and what was approved in Prague must not be tolerated in Vienna. It was at Prague that Paganini actually published this letter from his mother as proof that he was not the son of the devil !

DEAREST SON,—At last, after seven months have elapsed since I wrote to you at Milan, I had the happiness of receiving your letter of the 9th current, through the intermediary of Signor Agnino, and was much rejoiced to find that you were in the enjoyment of good health. I am also delighted to find that, after your travels to Paris and London, you purpose visiting Genoa expressly to embrace

* This letter was published in *The Quarterly Musical Magazine an Review*.

me. I assure you, my prayers are daily offered up to the Most High, that my health may be sustained, also yours, so that my desire may be realised.

My dream has been fulfilled, and that which God promised me has been accomplished. Your name is great, and art, with the help of God, has placed you in a position of independence. Beloved, esteemed by your fellow citizens, you will find in my bosom and those of your friends, that repose which your health demands.

The portraits which accompanied your letter have given me great pleasure. I had seen in the papers all the accounts you give me of yourself. You may imagine, as your mother, what an infinite source of joy it was to me. Dear son, I entreat you to continue to inform me of all that concerns you, for with this assurance I shall feel that it will prolong my days, and be convinced that I shall still have the happiness of embracing you.

We are all well. In the name of your relations, I thank you for the sums of money you have sent. Omit nothing that will render your name immortal. Eschew the vices of great cities, remembering that you have a mother who loves you affectionately, and whose fondest aspirations are your health and happiness. She will never cease her supplications to the All-powerful for your preservation.

Embrace your amiable companion for me, and kiss little Achille. Love me as I love you.

Your ever affectionate mother,

21st July, 1828.   TERESA PAGANINI.

From Prague, Paganini went to Berlin, where he remained four months. He was received with the utmost enthusiasm, and on the evening of his first concert he exclaimed: " I have found my Vienna public again." Wherever Paganini stayed for any length of time it suddenly became the fashion to learn to play the violin ; and the fair members of the aristocratic families were among the most eager to become pupils of the famous man. Paganini made a great deal of money in Berlin. The critics were divided in opinion as to his merits ; but

Rellstab, whom Schumann once called "Wretched Berlinese reviewer," was favourably impressed. Paganini is said to have received a challenge from Baron Sigismond von Praun, to a public contest for supremacy in performance, but as the would-be opponent was a youth of seventeen, Paganini disdained him. Perhaps he thought of his own presumption in his young days! Paganini's tour was one continual triumphal progress. At Königsberg his first concert realised about £330, an unprecedented sum in that place; at Frankfort his four concerts produced something like £1,000. A critic wrote of him: "One striking peculiarity of his playing is the extraordinary effect it produces on persons wholly devoid of musical cultivation. Most *virtuosi* play only for the learned; not so Paganini. His performance is alike appreciated by men of business and connoisseurs, by children and grown persons—it is felt and understood by all. This is the distinctive characteristic of all that is great in art."

He was at Leipzig in 1829, and was among the visitors at the house of Abraham Mendelssohn—the pleasant garden-house in the Leipziger Strasse—and his portrait figures in Hensel's collection. In June, 1830, Paganini was in Cassel, when Spohr heard him for the first time— of which more later. In Hamburg the same year Heine heard him, and his vivid and extraordinary notice of the artist must be briefly quoted. " I believe," said Heine, " that only one man has succeeded in putting Paganini's true physiognomy upon paper—a deaf painter, Lyser by name, who in a frenzy full of genius has with a few

strokes of chalk so well hit the great violinist's head that
one is at tbe same time amused and terrified at the truth
of the drawing. 'The devil guided my hand,' the deaf
painter said to me, chuckling mysteriously, and nodding
his head with a good-natured irony in the way he generally accompanied his genial witticisms. . . . . The
Hamburg Opera House was the scene of this concert,
and the art-loving public had flocked there so early, and
in such numbers, that I only just succeeded in obtaining
a little place in the orchestra." Then he goes on to
describe the audience and the entrance of Paganini.
" Is that a man brought into the arena at the moment of
death, like a dying gladiator, to delight the public
with his convulsions ?   Or is it one risen from the dead,
a vampire with a violin, who, if not the blood out of our
hearts, at any rate sucks the gold out of our pockets ?
Such questions crossed our minds while Paganini was
performing his strange bows, but all those thoughts were
at once still when the wonderful master placed his violin
under his chin and began to play.   As for me, you already
know my musical second-sight, my gift of seeing at each
tone a figure equivalent to the sound, and so Paganini
with each stroke of his bow brought visible forms and
situations before my eyes; he told me in melodious
hieroglyphics all kinds of brilliant tales ; he, as it were,
made a magic lantern play its coloured antics before me,
he himself being chief actor. . . .   A holy, ineffable
ardour dwelt in the sounds, which often trembled, scarce
audibly, in mysterious whisper on the water, then swelled
out again with a shuddering sweetness, like a bugle's

notes heard by moonlight, and then finally poured forth in unrestrained jubilee, as if a thousand bards had struck their harps and raised their voices in a song of victory." Thus, a poet on a poet in tones.

In 1829 Paganini was in Warsaw, and Chopin was among those who heard him. As he was leaving, in July, he was stopped some distance from the city by a numerous company who had met together in a garden. They drank the health of the artist, and Joseph Xaver Elsner, Director of the Conservatoire, handed him a costly snuff box, bearing this inscription: "Al Cavaliere Nicolo Paganini, gli ammiratori del suo talento, Varsovia 19 Luglio 1829." Paganini pressed it to his lips, speechless with surprise, and affected almost to tears. At Munich he gave three concerts in November of the same year; and at the close of the last *soirée* the artist was crowned by Stunz, the Kapellmeister, while thousands of laudatory poems were showered from different parts of the hall. At Stuttgart, the King of Würtemberg presented him with 100 *louis d'or*, and it is said that before leaving Germany Paganini sent over £6,000 to the Bank of England for safe custody, a proceeding which showed his good sense, and perhaps revealed a mistrust of his continental friends.

Paganini's tours, extending over three years, embraced Bohemia, Poland, Saxony, Bavaria, Prussia, and the Rhine provinces. Many more details might be given, but they are really needless: it was always the same story of the artist's success, excepting, indeed, at Augsburg, where the criticisms were adverse, as at Prague.

An anecdote may fitly close the narration of Paganini's long stay in Germany, as it reveals an interesting trait in the character of the peasantry. Paganini, in the autumn of 1829, was summoned to appear before the Queen Dowager of Bavaria, at the Castle of Tegernsee, a magnificent residence of the Kings of Bavaria, situated on the banks of a lake of the same name. At the moment the concert was about to begin, a great bustle was heard outside. The Queen, having enquired the cause, was informed that about sixty of the neighbouring peasantry, having been told of the arrival of the famous Italian violinist, were come with the hope of hearing some of his notes, and requested that the windows should be opened, in order that they also might enjoy his talent. The Queen went beyond their wishes, and with truly Royal good-nature, gave orders that they should all be admitted into the saloon, where she had the pleasure of remarking their discernment, and the judicious manner in which they applauded the most striking parts of the distinguished artist's performance.

Frankfort seems to have been a favourite stopping place with Paganini, and from there, at last, he quitted the fatherland, and arrived at Strasburg, where he gave two concerts, and thence proceeded direct to Paris.

It has to be observed that France had just been through another Revolution, and the turmoil, social and political, had not subsided. To a populace seething in this fevered atmosphere anything by way of diversion would be welcome. The man of the hour was Paganini, for in a sense he combined within himself the surrounding elements and influences. At the moment the public was just in the mood for Paganini, and the artist met the craving for excitement. He gave his first concert in the Opera House on March 9th, 1831, and notwithstanding that the prices of admission were tripled, the house was crammed. It would be impossible, says Fétis, to describe the enthusiasm with which the audience were seized when listening to the extraordinary artist, an enthusiasm approaching delirium, frenzy. Paganini's Studies had long been known to Parisian violinists, but they remained enigmas impossible of solution. At his third concert, March 25th, Paganini introduced a new concerto, in D minor, which, like so much of his music, is lost. In Paris the infamous persecution of the artist seems to have reached its climax. Fétis states that Paris was above all places hostile to Paganini, although that city had contributed more than any other place to the *éclat* of his success. His portrait was on every wall, and exhibited in the windows of print shops. Paganini himself stopped to look at one representing him in prison ; and while scanning it with some amusement, found he was being surrounded by a crowd who were scrutinising him with close interest, evidently comparing his features with those of the lithograph. This was too much, and Paganini sought his friend Fétis, and confided to him his troubles, seeking his aid for their amelioration. Fétis requested Paganini to supply him with particulars, and then indited a long epistle, which, signed by Paganini, appeared in the *Revue Musicale*. Quotation may be deferred until the narration of Paganini's public career is completed, and a more detailed consideration of the character of the man and the artist is entered upon.

One incident that occurred during Paganini's visit to Paris may be related. The officers of the different legions of the National Guard combined to organise a grand ball to be held in the Opera House for the benefit of the poor. They thought it would add greatly to the attractions of the function if they could prevail upon Paganini to attend and play a few pieces. To ask for violin solos in a place prepared for a ball, and among an assemblage met for dancing, argued a very curious taste, or want of it. Paganini owed it to his dignity as an artist to refuse the invitation, which he did. For this he was bitterly assailed by a section of the press, and was compelled to publish a letter justifying himself.* He explained that he had already given up the Opera House, which was at his disposal, for the preparations for the ball, and that involved the loss of receipts for one concert—from 15,000 to 20,000 francs. He added that in Berlin, Vienna, and all the towns where he had continued any time, he made it a duty to perform for the benefit of the unfortunate; and he certainly should not leave Paris without devoting the proceeds of one of his *soirées* to the relief of the poor of that capital. He kept his word; gave the promised concert, and the poor profited by a refusal that was attributed to him as a crime.

Berlioz, then in Italy—he had just won the Grand Prix de Rome—passing through a crisis in his life,

---

* Addressed to *Le Corsaire*, and reproduced (in English) in *The Globe*.

stayed a few days in Genoa. In his autobiography he
wrote: "All Paris was raving about Paganini, while I,
with my usual luck, was kicking my heels in his native
town instead of listening to him. I tried to gather some
information about their distinguished townsman from the
Genoese, but found that, like other people engaged in
commerce, they cared little for the fine arts, and spoke quite
'indifferently of the genius whom Germany, France and
England had received with open arms. They could not
even show me his father's house." So quickly and easily
can one be forgotten! England had not yet received
Paganini, but it was many years after this time that
Berlioz penned his autobiography.

Liszt, in Paris, his first dream of love cruelly dispelled,
shunned the world and buried himself in seclusion. For
the time the artist within him was dead, and his thoughts
turned to the priesthood. The revolution of 1830 awoke
him. The Magyar blood was aroused, and sympathising
with the people's struggles Liszt planned a *Symphonie
révolutionnaire*. But it was Paganini who, the next year,
touched Liszt as it were with a magic wand, and gave
the direction to the genius and energy of the young artist.
Of this more in its proper place. Early in May, 1831,
Paganini left Paris for London.

CHAPTER V.

FÉTIS stated that Paganini's visit to London excited the most lively curiosity, but did not awake that intelligent interest which welcomed him in the Capital of France. This does not sound complimentary to London, but perhaps Fétis read some of the introductory comments of the press when Paganini was about to reach our shores. This is a specimen: " We shall talk of Paganini very much till he comes. When he arrives nobody will speak or think of anything else for nine, perhaps eighteen, days : he will be everywhere: all other violinists will be utterly forgotten: it will be agreed that the instrument was never before heard; that his predecessors were all tyros; all other fiddles mere kits. There will be Paganini rondos and waltzes; variations, long, short, hard, easy, all *à la Paganini*. We shall have Paganini hats, caps, etc., and the hair of all the beaux patronised by beauty, will be after his curious pattern. His influence will extend to our tables, and there will be Paganini puffs served up daily. Then, all at once, his very name will cease to be pronounced by persons of *ton*; and, as a matter of course, people not of *ton*—not of the Devonshire circle, not of Almack's—will imitate those

Plate VI.—See Appendix.—TITLE-PAGE OF COMIC SONG, 1831.

who are : and the Italian player, like the penultimate fashion, will be utterly forgotten!—*in good society.* I will even allow him to flourish here two whole months, provided no new chin-chopper* arrive in the interim, no *danseuse* with a miraculous toe, to contest the supremacy of his wonderful bow : should any such rival enter the lists with him, his glory will set in less than a moon, and never blaze again above our fashionable horizon."†

Here is another from *The Examiner* :—" There cannot be a more inoffensive creature. His sole propensity is to gain money by his art, and his passion to lose it at the gambling table. Paganini's bow (*Scottice*, boo) is almost as wonderful as his bow *(Anglice*, fiddle-stick)—the crawfish would attempt something like it were he on the stage, but not so well."

Well, we've improved in manners 'somewhat since 1831. No respectable paper would publish now such notices in advance of any distinguished artist, however eccentric he might be. Paganini duly arrived in London in May, 1831. His first concert was announced for the 21st in this manner :

THE KING'S THEATRE.

SIGNOR PAGANINI respectfully informs the Nobility, Subscribers, and Frequenters of the Opera, and the public, that he will give a GRAND MISCELLANEOUS

---

* An allusion to Michael Boai, whose performances in London, in 1830, were of a curious description,—producing tones by merely striking his chin !

† The Dilettante, in *The Harmonicon*, VIII, 479.

CONCERT of Vocal and Instrumemtal Music, at this theatre, To-morrow Evening.

Prices of Boxes:—Pit Tier, 8 Guineas; Grand Tier, 10 Guineas; One Pair, 9 Guineas; Two Pair, 6 Guineas; Three Pair, 4 Guineas; Stalls, 2 Guineas; Orchestra, 1½ Guineas; Admission to the Pit, 1 Guinea; Ditto to the Gallery, Half a Guinea.

This announcement produced a storm of indignation. Articles appeared in *The Times, The Courier, The Observer, The Chronicle*, and correspondence of a heated character was carried on. The editor of *The Harmonicon*, calculated that a full house at the prices would realise more than 3,000 guineas, and M. Laporte, the manager of the King's Theatre, was virtually accused of conspiring to rob the public. It must be explained that Laporte "farmed" Paganini; and as the latter invariably doubled the ordinary prices of admission, his impressario naturally desired to share in the golden harvest. Laporte wrote to *The Times* a hurried note on May 19th, at eleven p.m., stating that at some future time he would refute the charges brought against him; and the next day a letter from Paganini to Laporte, and advertised in the newspaper, gave pause to the wordy warfare. It was as follows :—

Sir,   *Friday*, 29th May.

Finding myself too unwell, I request you will respectfully inform the public that the Concert announced for to-morrow will not take place.

Your obedient Servant,

To M. Laporte.   Nicolo Paganini.

Paganini was in a wretched state of health when he reached London, and his condition was not improved by the turmoil his announcement had created. The terms of his contract with Laporte were published in *The Observer*, and it was shown that Paganini had practically surrendered his freedom of action. This may be illustrated by a story that I have not met with in any English publication, though it may be true all the same. It is from the notice of Paganini in Mendel's " Musikalisches Conversations-Lexikon." His Majesty William IV. sent to enquire what honorarium Paganini required to play at the Court. Paganini answered : £100, a mere bagatelle. As the messenger tendered him one half that sum, Paganini haughtily replied, " His Majesty can hear me at a much cheaper rate if he will attend my concert. But my terms are not left for me to settle."

The concert postponed from May 21st was then announced for June 3rd, but the question of the high prices had yet to be disposed of. Conflicting statements were made—one to the effect that Paganini expressed his regret that they had not been fixed still higher! Be that as it may, that was not the time to trifle with an angry public. There was not a moment to be lost, and some one must give way. The matter was soon decided. On June 2nd, appeared in *The Courier* and *The Globe* the translation of a letter from Paganini, which may be reproduced for the sake of its contents :

" The time appointed for my first Concert at the King's Theatre so nearly approaches, that I feel it my duty to announce it myself, and to claim the favour of the English

nation, which honours the arts as much as I respect her.
Having been accustomed in all the towns of the Continent to double the usual prices at the theatres where I
have given my Concerts, and, but little acquainted with
the customs of this Capital, where I present myself for
the first time, I thought I might do the same here. But
having been informed by several papers that the existing
prices here are higher than those on the Continent, and
having myself ascertained that the statement was correct,
I willingly second the wish of a public whose esteem and
protection I desire as my greatest recompense.

    (Signed)   NICOLO PAGANINI.

       London, June 1st, 1831."

At last the concert took place in the King's Theatre,
June 3rd, 1831. There was an orchestra erected on the
stage. Many musicians have left a record of the extraordinary impression made by Paganini on that occasion,
and have attempted to describe the man. In the present
place quotation may be limited to the remarks of the
editor of *The Harmonicon*, William Ayrton, a cultivated
musician, and a sober-minded critic. He wrote thus:
" The long, laboured, reiterated articles relative to Paganini, in all the foreign journals for years past, have
spoken of his powers as so astonishing, that we were
quite prepared to find them fall far short of report; but
his performances at his first concert, on the 3rd of last
month, convinced us that it is possible to exceed the most
sanguine expectation, and to surpass what the most
eulogistic writers have asserted. We speak, however,
let it be understood, in reference to his powers of execu-

Plate VII.—See Appendix.

tion solely. These are little less than marvellous, and such as we could only have believed on the evidence of our own senses; they imply a strong natural propensity to music, with an industry, a perseverance, a devotedness, and also a skill in inventing means, without any parallel in the history of his instrument."

So far, the musician. The critics on the press may also have been musicians, though at that time it was not usual to have a musical department, if such a term may pass, in the daily or weekly papers. *The Athenæum*, in its notice, does not reveal the polished style of a high-class literary journal. This is how it deals with the concert: —" At length all differences have been arranged, and the *mighty wonder* has come forth—a very Zamiel in appearance, and certainly a very devil in performance! He is, beyond rivalry, the *bow* ideal of fiddling faculty! He possesses a demon-like influence over his instrument, and makes it utter sounds almost superhuman. . . . The arrival of this magician is quite enough to make the greater part of the fiddling tribe commit suicide."

And now let us turn to the concert itself. The fashionable world did not rush to the theatre, and only two boxes were let. The stalls and orchestra were full, and also the pit, but not crowded. The audience consisted in great part of musicians; and even those engaged in the orchestra were listeners for the first time, as Paganini at rehearsal only played such passages as served for "cues," and in nowise revealed his powers.

The object of a great *virtuoso* would naturally be an exhibition of his own talent, but Paganini was not

prodigal of his playing at the first concert. He had
engaged the orchestra of the Philharmonic Society, then
probably the finest in Europe, and his programme opened
with Beethoven's Symphony, No. 2, in D. It will be
shown later that Paganini had a great veneration for
Beethoven. Then Signor Lablache was the solo vocalist,
so Paganini was in the best of company. His first piece
was the Concerto in E flat*, and his second solo the
Military Sonata for the G string, the theme being
Mozart's " Non più andrai." The receipts were £700.
Paganini had a most flattering reception, and his performances were greeted with acclamations, and waving of
hats and handkerchiefs. The members of the orchestra
were astounded. Mori avowed that if he could not
sell, he would at least burn, his fiddle; Lindley, who
stammered terribly, said that " it was the d-d-devil ";
and Dragonetti (whose " he's were " she's ") growled out,
" She's mighty esprit ! " Cramer thanked heaven that he
was not a violinist. A striking feature of Paganini's performance was his playing from memory. The *Athenænm*
remarked, " He plays without a reading desk or book
stand ; this gives an air of *improvising* to his performance,
which we hope to see imitated, if any one be found hardy
enough to undertake a violin solo for the next seven
years." No violinist would venture to play a concerto
now with the music before him, but he may not be aware
that it was Paganini who set the fashion of playing
without book.

---

* Now played in D.

The public now forgot all about the trouble of the high prices, and the second concert, given in the same place on the 10th, was so well attended that the receipts were about £1,200. On this occasion Paganini played his Concerto in B minor, and Lablache struck the little silver bell in the Rondo. He also gave his variations on "The Carnival of Venice," and a Sonata on the fourth string, in which the Prayer from *Mosè in Egitto* was introduced. The third concert took place on the 13th, when Paganini brought out another new Concerto. Something like £900 was realised. At the fourth concert, on the 16th, Paganini played a *Cantabile* on two strings, a *Rondo Scherzoso*, by Rodolphe Kreutzer—a detail to be noticed,—a *Larghetto gajo*, the Military Sonata, and the variations on "Non più mesta," from Rossini's *La Cenerentola*. The fifth and last Concert was on the 22nd, when the house was crowded to excess, and the enthusiasm greater than ever.

But Paganini, or his astute manager, began to presume a little too much on the good nature of the public. Parting was "such sweet sorrow," that, like another Juliet, Paganini was inclined to prolong that process as long as possible. Final concerts succeeded each other —much like the "Farewells" of popular singers—until the audiences began to dwindle. At one, at the King's Theatre on July 4th, Paganini played a new Concerto in E major, "all expression and grace," and by far the best proof given of his talent since his arrival in London. Paganini gave two concerts at the London Tavern in July. The first was well attended, but at the second there

was no orchestra. The concert was a failure— " and no
wonder, for the Signor tried an experiment on the for-
bearance of the citizens, and actually took only a pianist
and one or two second-rate singers with him to make up a
half-guinea concert! This was too much even for John
Bull to submit to."*

What a curious side-light this shows upon concert
matters in the first half of the nineteenth century! Now-
a-days the " experiment " is for the *virtuoso* to engage an
orchestra.†

Paganini played at some of the benefit concerts during
the season, taking one-third of the gross receipts. There
was evidently ill-feeling on this point, for Lablache and
Rubini now refused to sing where Paganini played. It
was said, even, that the leader of his orchestra had to
sue Paganini for recovery of his fees, but the artist in
question, Spagnoletti, put the matter right by publicly
stating that his action was against M. Laporte, and
that against Signor Paganini he had never had the
slightest cause of complaint. Time was found for a few
provincial visits. In July Paganini gave two concerts
at Cheltenham, and .there he got into trouble. It was
announced that his engagements would not permit his
remaining beyond the second day. His concerts were
well supported, and one of the Subscription Balls, at
the Rotunda, was relinquished in order that no hindrance

---

* Harmonicon, IX. p. 190

† At that time concert givers always engaged an orchestra, but
the gigantic combinations of the present day were, of course,
unknown, and unnecessary.

should stand in the way of those desirous of hearing
the violinist. But when it was given out that Paganini
would give a third performance, there was a disturbance.
Some leading residents had a handbill printed calling
upon the "nobility and gentry" to support the established
amusements of the town, by patronizing the Ball, if only
as an act of justice to the proprietor. The effect was to
secure a thronged attendance at the Rotunda, and so
poor an assemblage at the theatre, that Paganini refused
to perform. Of course the manager had to communicate
this unpleasant piece of information to the audience, at
the same time offering to return the admission money;
but the people were in no pacific frame of mind, and
they marched straightway to the hotel where Paganini
was staying, and demanded the fulfilment of his engagement. A mob soon collected, and their demeanour
became so threatening that there was nothing left but
compliance with their demand. Paganini went to the
theatre, played two of his most favourite pieces with
great success, and at midnight posted off for London.
It appeared that he had agreed to perform for two-thirds
of the receipts, but finding the house not half full,
demanded two hundred guineas in advance. This the
local manager refused, and informed the audience of the
fact; and the outbreak was the natural result. The local
paper remarked: "We believe this is the only instance
as yet upon record of Paganini's playing to empty benches,
and himself unpaid." Paganini addressed a letter to the
Times, giving another version of the incident, but he did
not appear to have come out of the affair very well.

His manager's share in the business may be left to conjecture.

One other little circumstance seems to have caused a certain amount of irritation. Paganini was engaged for the Lord Mayor's banquet at the Mansion House on July 9th. When the Lord Mayor proposed the toast of the Lord Chancellor, before Lord Brougham's rising to return thanks, Paganini played a solo. He evidently displaced the usual glee party, but in any case it was not the most artistic function to assist at, and money must have been the chief consideration.

Paganini carried his London concerts into August, and visited Norwich, where again a third performance took place when only two were announced. The local manager was a heavy loser, as Paganini (or his agent) had arranged for a specific sum, and there was very little in excess for the payment of vocalists, and general expenses. There was also a clashing with an important fixture at the theatre, and feeling ran high, though there was no violent demonstration as at Cheltenham. Towards the end of August, Paganini set out for Dublin, being engaged for the first Musical Festival held in that city.

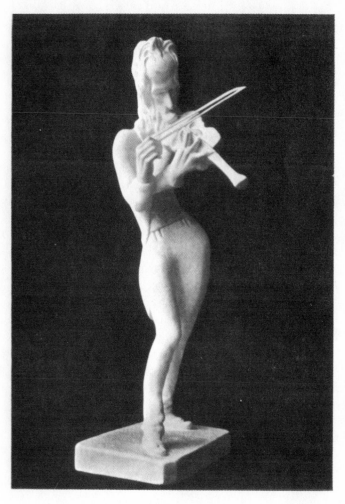

Plate VIII.—See Appendix.

THE CELEBRATED STATUETTE (CARICATURE),
BY DAINTON.

CHAPTER VI.

DUBLIN held her first Musical Festival from August 30th to September 3rd, 1831, and in connection with this event, it is interesting to note, Henry Fothergill Chorley contributed his first musical criticism to the *Athenæum.** There was very little about Paganini, but much about the oratorio, "The Triumph of Faith," of Ferdinand Ries. It may be observed, in passing, that in the first half of the nineteenth century musical festivals were more numerous than they are now—there were five in 1831. With the exception of those given in York Minster (1823-1835), they were not on the large scale of the principal present day celebrations; but they were relatively of more importance, inasmuch as there were then fewer musical centres beyond the metropolis, and small towns would have had little music but for those periodic gatherings.

Dublin's scheme was ambitious ; for Paganini's fees for the three evening concerts was 500 guineas. Braham and Henry Phillips were among the vocalists engaged, and the latter, in his " Musical Recollections," gives a

---

* Chorley, then living in Liverpool, had previously sent some short pieces in verse to that paper, but did not become a member of its staff until 1833.

very interesting and amusing account of Paganini at the festival. No one seemed to know how Paganini arrived in Dublin, which gave rise to a vague idea that he was wafted across by the *Flying Dutchman*. Where he lodged was equally a mystery. He arrived at the stage door of the Theatre Royal on the evening of the first concert, and immediately ordered an apartment to be got ready, and the room to be perfectly darkened. There he paced up and down, playing snatches of his music until the time for his *début* before a Dublin audience.

The Theatre was crammed to suffocation. The Lord Lieutenant and his Suite attended in State, and all the *élite* of Dublin were in the dress tier. When the Conductor, Sir George Smart, led Paganini to the centre of the stage there was a terrific outburst of applause, followed by breathless silence, as the great artist went through his deliberate process of adjusting his violin, raising his bow, and letting it rest upon the strings before commencing. This was too trying to the mercurial temperament of the occupants of the gallery, and before many seconds there was a stentorian shout, " Well ! we're all ready ! " The house was convulsed with laughter, peal after peal rang through the theatre. Paganini, stamping with rage, turned to Sir George Smart, and cried, " *Qu'est ce que c'est ?* " The explanation seemed to make matters worse, and Paganini left the orchestra. Some time elapsed before he could be induced to return; but when he did so, and began to play, he created the same effect as elsewhere. The next day everybody was exclaiming: " Ah ! sure, have you heard the Paganini; och murther! and his fiddle?" Such is the account Henry Phillips gives, but it is not easy to attach credence to all he has put in his book.

At one of the concerts Paganini played the concerto in B minor, with the Rondo *à la clochette,* when an excited Hibernian shouted above the storm of applause, "Arrah now, Signor Paganini, have a drop of whiskey, darling, and ring the bell again!" Paganini's departure from Dublin was as mysterious as his arrival. On his return to London he failed to attract much attention, and seems to have been mostly on tour in the provinces and in Scotland. One incident in London was so singular that it deserves mention. Carlyle was supposed to have taken a walk with Paganini. Fancy "the Sage of Chelsea" in company with "the magician of the bow"! Thomas Carlyle was in London in 1831 vainly negotiating for the publication of "Sartor Resartus." One day his friend, Edward Irving, took him to Belgrave Square to dine with Henry Drummond. They walked along Piccadilly, thronged with fashionable promenaders; and as both men were of peculiar personal appearance, they doubtless attracted some attention. This is what Carlyle subsequently wrote:—"Irving, I heard afterward, was judged, from the broad hat, brown skin, and flowing black hair, to be in all probability the one-string fiddler, Paganini—a tall, lean, taciturn abstruse-looking figure—who was then, after his sort, astonishing the idle of mankind."* Carlyle has said many true, and many

---

* "Reminiscences," by Thomas Carlyle, I., 311.

beautiful things about music, but one may search his
writings in vain for a good word about musicians!

In December of this year (1831) Paganini was
announced to play in Bristol. The following "squib" or
lampoon was issued :—

PAGANINI.

To the Citizens of Bristol.

Fellow Citizens,—It is with feelings of unqualified disgust
that I witness the announcement of Signor Paganini's Performance to take place in this City: Why at this period of Distress?
With the recollection of so many scenes of misery still fresh in our
minds, and whilst Subscriptions are required to the extent of our
means in order to Feed and Clothe the Poor: why is this
Foreign Fiddler now to appear? for the purpose of draining
those resources which would be infinitely better applied in the
exercise of the best feeling of man—Charity. Do not suffer your-
selves to be imposed upon by the Payment of Charges which are well
worthy the name of extortion ; rather suffer under the imputation
of a want of Taste than support any of the tribe of Foreign
Music-Monsters, who collect the Cash of this Country and waft it
to their own shores, laughing at the infatuation of John Bull.

December 10th, 1831.   PHILADELPHUS.

A. Saint. Typ. Castle Printing Office, 54, Castle Street, Bristol.

Paganini's concerts at Leeds, early in 1832, were so
well managed that, out of the profits, a liberal donation
was presented to the fund for the relief of the poor. At
Birmingham, in February of that year, his visit caused
such an influx of strangers to the town, that neither
lodgings nor stabling could meet the demand made upon
them. A popular song was written for the occasion, and
the streets rang with it long after the violinist had left
the place. Two lines ran thus :—

> " It's well worth a guinea to see Paganini,
> To see how he curls his hair."

At Brighton some time earlier, the high prices were nearly causing a riot, through the issue of an inflammatory placard against them. Mr. William Gutteridge, a well-known musician of that place, who had arranged for the concerts, had to ask the protection of the magistrates, but fortunately no outbreak occurred. The squabbles about prices, the charges of avarice brought against Paganini, and the acrimonious tone of part of the press, afford melancholy reading. His gains were said to reach £20,000. In March, 1832, he left London for Paris. There, he gave a concert for the poor on March 18th. He did not stay very long in France, and on his way again to this country, occurred the incident referred to as one of the indignities to which he was subjected. This is the story.

Paganini having to pass through Boulogne on his way to England, decided to give a concert in that town, which boasted of a Philharmonic Society. Paganini deputed a friend to arrange for that Society to assist at the concert.

All seemed going well until Paganini arrived on the scene, when the amateurs stipulated for a certain number of free admissions for their friends and families, as a recognition for their assistance. Paganini represented to them that in a small concert room so many free admissions would leave little room for the paying public, and he could not accede to their demand. However, they would not give way, so Paganini declared his intention to engage a professional band. This did not suit the views of the amateurs, and they threatened the professional players

with the loss of patronage and pupils if they dared assist
Paganini ; and the unfortunate artists, dependent as they
were upon that support, had to refuse the offer made
them. But Paganini was not to be baffled ; he determined to give the concert, and to perform without any
accompaniment at all. This he did ; and now came the
ludicrous sequel. A number of those amateurs actually
paid for admission to the concert, on purpose to hiss the
independent artist. This they did as soon as he entered
the concert-room. Despising such petty spite, Paganini
entrusted his revenge to his art, and the rapturous plaudits
of the audience proper soon reduced to a pitiable silence
those who had offered so gross an insult. As a writer
said at the time : " The amateurs of Boulogne have
earned for themselves a niche in the history of the art—
they have *hissed* Paganini."

To digress, for a moment. Paganini's performance,
solus, was a recital pure and simple; perhaps the first
ever given in a concert room. In Grove's " Dictionary
of Music and Musicians " there is this definition : " Recital,
a term which has come into use in England to signify a
performance of solo music by one instrument and one
performer." It was probably first used by Liszt, in
1840, when he advertised his performances as " Recitals."
The first was given at the Hanover Square Rooms, on
June 9th, and was called by the *Musical World* a curious
exhibition. The "one man show," as the recital has
been irreverently termed, may not conduce to the
highest interest of art, but Paganini—not Liszt—was its
inventor.

G. Rossini   Nicolò Paganini   J Gasta

PLATE 9. (*See Appendix.*)

Paganini made his *rentrée* at Covent Garden Theatre on July 6th, but he did not appear to have played anything new. Neither did he attract much attention, and little need be said respecting his visit. He was back again in London in 1833, but was out of favour, and was advised to postpone his concerts until the public anger, caused by his refusal to play for the distressed English actors in Paris, had subsided. His first concert was given in the King's Theatre, on June 21st, when apparently he played nothing new, and had but a small audience. The press in general appeared to be hostile— the *Athenæum* did not notice him at all—and it is probable that his stay was not prolonged. He was in Paris later in the year, and was present at the concert given by Berlioz on the 22nd of December, when he heard the *Symphonie Fantastique*, and was so impressed that he wished Berlioz to write a solo for the wonderful Stradivari viola he possessed.*

Between Paganini and Berlioz there was a mutual attraction. Both had something of the volcanic in their nature; both did much battling with the hostile outer world. But more of their friendship later.

Paganini was in London once more in 1834, and gave a concert at the Adelphi Theatre on April 7th. Again nothing new, according to report. The next morning he gave a second concert at the Hanover Square Rooms, at which it was said not more than one hundred persons were present, and half of those went in with free tickets.

* Which resulted in the Symphony, "Harold in Italy," with a solo part for the viola.

The erstwhile popular idol was now dethroned. Paganini fell ill after this, and postponed his third concert.

The *Athenæum* referred to Paganini's playing to crowded houses at the Adelphi, and empty benches at the Hanover Square Rooms, and then went on to say: "His performance on the *Viol di Gamba*,* or some such instrument, is yet to come as is also a duet with Dragonetti, which, we are told, is to be the *ne plus ultra* of what is beautiful and amazing. He has, hitherto, only repeated his best compositions, and, as before, left every other violinist, ancient and modern, at an inconceivable distance behind him." This concert was to be the last, which induced the writer of the *Athenæum* notice to attend it. He found the "new instrument" nothing but a full-sized viola, tuned in the ordinary way. "Considering the difference of stop between this and the violin, his precision and brilliancy upon the former, as displayed in double stop passages, harmonics, and *arpeggi*, of extraordinary difficulty, were most amazing. . . . . In his grand concerto in E flat, his cadenza was one of the most wonderful combinations of novel harmony, and passages of execution, we ever heard." Apparently the duet with Dragonetti was not played, as nothing was said of it.

The directors of the music at the Oxford Commemoration week, May, 1834, were anxious to add Paganini's

---

* The spelling betrays an ignorance of the instrument, though the writer must have been Chorley himself. Interest in those antique instruments had not then been revived, nor were there artists to play upon them.

name to the attractions offered. He was approached,
accordingly, and, through his manager, announced his
terms—one thousand pounds. Astounded by the answer,
the Oxford Delegate desired that it might be committed
to writing. This was done, but when shown to Paganini,
he directed that guineas should be substituted for pounds.
He knew that art was not commerce! There is no
record of his playing at Oxford.

This last visit of Paganini to England had a romantic
termination. He had separated from Signora Bianca on
account of her jealous temper, and had fallen in love
with a young English girl—that is if current report may
be trusted. He proposed, for the purpose of securing
her a proper legal settlement, that the marriage should
take place in Paris, and he left London on June 26th,
arranging for her to follow him to Boulogne. The
young lady secretly left her home, but her father had his
suspicions, and apparently arrived at Boulogne first, for
the daughter, instead of meeting Paganini, was con-
fronted, on landing, by her father, with whom she
returned home. There is no doubt as to the occurrence,
for it was "in the papers," and names were given.
Schilling, whose *Encyclopædia* was published in 1837,
gives a long account of the affair, which he would not
have done had there been no truth in it, even though the
law of libel was not then very stringent. Here it will
suffice to say that the young lady was the daughter of a
man with whom Paganini lodged, and who was associated
with the concert work of the artist. Moreover, the girl
herself had, it would seem, sung at some of the con-

certs, and had become fascinated with the great violinist.

The incident might be passed over, only for the fact that to it was owing the impression that Paganini visited America before returning to Italy. Dubourg, in the later editions of his work "The Violin," states that Paganini spent part of his time in America, previous to his return to Italy in 1834. Now George Dubourg was a contemporary of Paganini, and his statement is not to be dismissed lightly, though he offers no evidence in support of it. At the present time it is difficult to find proof, one way or the other. The American papers in 1835 were speculating as to the birthplace of Paganini, and some of the explanations were meant to be funny, but are too vapid for repetition now. The *Musical World* for August 4th, 1837, in quoting an anecdote concerning Paganini's kindness to a poor musician, ends by saying Paganini took the poor man with him to America. The question was raised in the *Musical World* for January the 9th, 1886, and decided in the negative. The legend had this slender foundation. In the early part of 1835, the young lady whom Paganini wished to marry, went to the United States—she was an actress and vocalist of moderate ability—but her stay was brief. Still, everbody wished to see her, for wherever she went she was looked upon as the heroine of a romantic episode, and her name was always coupled with Paganini's. The story of the elopement had been carried across the Atlantic by scandal's winged feet; and it was said that Paganini sent a special messenger to America to reopen negotiations on the

delicate subject—arrangements that came to nothing.
The agent might have been taken, by Dubourg, for the
principal—hence the mistake. Paganini never went to
America, neither did he again return to the shores of
Albion.

CHAPTER VII.

IN the summer of 1834, Paganini, after an absence of six years, returned to his native land. He was now a rich man, and he invested part of his fortune in landed property, purchasing, among others, the Villa Gajona, near Parma, which he made his home—the first he could really call his own, and he was in his fifty-second year! His health was irretrievably broken down; he suffered from consumption of the larynx, and was losing the power of speech. He now sought peace and quiet, and thought of preparing for publication a complete edition of his compositions, which, if he had accomplished it, might have led to the explanation of his alleged secret. In November, or December, Paganini gave a concert at Piacenza—on the very same boards where he almost began his brilliant career—for the benefit of the poor; this was the first time he had been heard in Italy since 1828. The year 1835, Paganini passed alternately at Genoa, Milan, and his villa near Parma. The cholera then raging at Genoa was the cause of the rumour of Paganini's death. The dread scourge had claimed him for a victim, it was said, and the Continental journals devoted columns to him in the form of obituary notices.

The only English contribution to the necrology of
Paganini known to me was written by Chorley in the
Athenæum. It is both interesting and curious : for Chorley
manages to squeeze in his account of Paganini at the
Dublin festival, which the editor evidently cut out in
1831. That scarcely concerns us now, though it relates
that the *furore* caused by Paganini's performance could
not be appeased until he had mounted the grand pianoforte, in order that the audience might obtain a better
view of his lank proportions! An extract from his notice
must be given. It begins thus :—" *E Morto* !—the words
which the silent and absorbed man murmured to himself,
in a tone of deep feeling, after listening to one of
Beethoven's magnificent symphonies, are now—alas !—
to be uttered sadly for their speaker—Paganini is
dead !

" We would fain believe that the newspaper reports are
in error. . . . Let us hope that the intelligence from
Genoa, received this week [September], that the artist
had been carried off by the sudden and fearful death of
cholera, may, by some happy chance, prove one of those
' mistakes which it gives them pleasure to contradict.'
But, should it not—then, indeed, may Music put on
sackcloth and sit in ashes for her High Priest ! " Then
follows an " appreciation," to use a modern expression,
to which reference may be made later.

Chorley was an impressionable young man, in his
twenty-third year, when he attended the Dublin festival,
and so excited did he become over Paganini's performances, that he gave vent to his feelings in verse. That

poem he now inserted in the *Athenæum*, "as a farewell to one whose like we shall never hear again!" There are really fine thoughts in the poem, and, though too long to quote in its entirety, a few stanzas may well be rescued from the periodical in which they are buried.

O Paganini!—most undoubted king
   Of St. Cecilia's flock, alive or dead,
Whether their pasture be of pipe, or string,
   Or mighty organ, which doth overspread
Ancient Cathedral aisles with flood of sound,—
     In all the wizard craft, matured by labour,
That doth the spirit move, delight, astound,
     Thou hast no peer—thou hast not even a neighbour,
     In the long lapse of years from Tubal Cain to Weber.

Sages have said, who read the book of night,
   That once each hundred years some meteor flares
Across the startled heavens with brilliant flight,
   Making strange tumults in the land of stars;
And, 'mid the realm of constellations vast,
     In steady splendour ever rolling on,
Sweeps far and wide with fierce and furious haste,
     Rushing from pole to distant pole anon;
     And, like the monarch's ghost—"'Tis here—'tis there—
       'tis gone!"

Thou dost to these, the meteor-born, belong,
   O mighty monarch of the strings and bow!
And though it were to do sweet Cupid wrong
   To call thee else like him—yet on thy brow,
And in thy curved lips and flashing eyes,
     His clearest seal hath god-like Genius set,
Who bade thee from the common herd arise
     And win thyself a crown—nor ever yet
     Hath Art her votary graced with brighter coronet.

O that a stately temple might be reared
  On some wide plain—and open to the sky—
Where all the great, the gifted, the revered
  Side close to side, ensepulchred might lie !
And there, where many a breeze at evening's close
  In solemn dirge around their tomb should sweep,
Should all the sons of melody repose,
    That pilgrims from afar might come and weep,
    And by their sainted dust a silent vigil keep !

And there together in renown should rest,
  The Italian minstrel of the broken heart ! *
And he whose Requiem for a spirit blest
  Was his own dirge—too early lost Mozart !
And he of the Messiah—and the flight
  Of Israel's children from their bonds abhorred,
When God was cloud by day, and fire by night !
    And he, who sung of darkness, at one word
    Bursting to light—and Earth created by its Lord !

And many more—with whom ungentle Time
  Forbids my weak and wandering verse to say ;
Save one great master-spirit, whom my rhyme
  Must pause to honour—for the meteor ray
Burnt with intensest radiance o'er his head ;
  Albeit too soon within his eager ear
The realm of sound deep silence overspread,
    Whom yet the world is learning to revere—
    Beethoven ! he should sleep with thee—the Wizard—near !

There's left a space, beside his hallowed dust,
  For thee with whom began my feeble song ;
But be it long before the encroaching rust
  Of Time wear out thy energies—and long
Ere the grim Tyrant with resistless call
  Beckon thee hence—before thy bow be hung
In some gray chapel—and thy brethren all
    Strive for thy magic instruments unstrung ;
    If Heaven were kind to man, thou shouldst be ever young !

* Pergolesi.

Plate X.—See Appendix.

COPY OF OIL PAINTING OF PAGANINI IN THE MUNICIPAL
MUSEUM AT GENOA.

A fortnight later, Chorley was able to reassure his readers by contradicting the report. It seems that the rumour was started through the death of Dr. Paganini (referred to at the beginning of this essay), and there seems little doubt but that he was the brother of the violinist.

In 1836, some speculators applied to Paganini to give the support of his name and his talent to the founding of a Casino in Paris, of which the ostensible object was music, the real end, gambling. It has been suggested that the project appealed to Paganini's avarice, which caused him to lend himself to the accomplishment of the undertaking. On the other hand, it is fair to assume that the artist was in ignorance of the true motive of the promoters of the scheme; and the fact that certain instructions to the trustees of the fortune settled on his son had been made public some four years earlier lends countenance to the impression that he was disgusted with gambling, and had long ceased to indulge in the vicious pastime.

In the early summer of 1837, Paganini's health having improved, he gave several concerts in Turin, both for the benefit of the poor, and on his own behalf. Later in the year, however, he was in Paris, living in the greatest seclusion. The CASINO PAGANINI was opened, apparently in October, 1837. The building was situated in the Rue Mont Blanc, and was supposed to be a kind of Club of Art and Literature. An orchestra of some fifty performers was engaged for concerts, which were open to subscribers only. In the grounds a brass band played to those assembled, and admission there apparently was free to the public. The object of the undertaking was not made known. A French paper stated by way of a joke that Paganini's part in the proceedings was to walk round the garden when the weather was fine. The Government refused to license the place as a gambling-house, and the management had to rely upon the concerts alone. It would appear that Paganini had signed a contract to play at the concerts, but the wretched state of his health was the excuse for his not doing so. He had been in Paris off and on from 1837 to some time in 1839. In 1838, certainly before April, he was there, and went to hear a newly invented instrument termed the Harmoniphone. This was the work of an ingenious musician, Jacques Reine Paris. It was a small key-board instrument designed to imitate the oboe, and intended as a substitute for it, in places where oboe players were not available. A distinguished company was invited to meet Paganini, who was greatly interested and pleased with the invention. Then, in December, Paganini witnessed what Berlioz described as the massacre of his " Benvenuto Cellini " at the opera. In the same month was inaugurated a society for the production of classical compositions, and for the encouragement of musical artists, and at this brilliant function, held in the Salle Erard, Paganini was present, with Meyerbeer, Auber, De Beriot, Donizetti, and a host of other celebrities. On the 16th of the month Paganini attended the concert given by Berlioz at the Conservatoire, when the symphony, " Harold," was performed. Paganini heard it for the first time, and at the close of

the concert occurred the affecting incident of Paganini
kneeling on the stage and kissing the hand of Berlioz,
the demonstration being followed by a magnificent
donation of 20,000 francs. Paganini seems to have had a
transient recovery, for the papers spoke of his becoming
corpulent.

Still, he did not play at the Casino Concerts, and a
crisis soon arose. Early in 1839, the directors of the
Casino brough an action against Paganini for breach of
contract, and he was decreed to pay damages to the
amount of 20,000 francs. This decision so much dis-
pleased both plaintiffs and defendant that they appealed
against it. The case did not come on again for some
time, and Paganini sought rest and change in the south
of France. He stayed for some time at Marseilles,
where, at the house of a friend, he once more abandoned
himself to his art, devoting his time alternately to his
violin and his guitar. Fétis states that notwithstanding
his feeble health, Paganini attended a performance of
Cherubini's *Requiem* for men's voices ; and on June 21st
went to one of the churches to take part in the performance of Beethoven's Mass in C.

But his malady could only be alleviated by frequent
change of clime. Accordingly, in October we find him at
Genoa, in the vain hope that his native air would prove
beneficial ; but he was prostrated by a violent nervous
attack almost immediately following his arrival. He
must, soon after, have left for Nice, which he never
quitted alive. Nice, though a pleasant place, was not
regarded as at all a favourable retreat for persons suffering

from pulmonary or bronchial affections, and it proved
fatal to the great artist. But we must, for the moment,.
return to Paris.

The rehearing of the Casino case came before the
Cour Royale, Paris, on January 3rd, 1840. Paganini
could not, of course, attend in person, but he was represented by Counsel, and it may be of interest to name the
man who was entrusted with his defence. It was a
certain Mons. Chaix-d'Est-Ange. From accounts of the
proceedings, this legal luminary addressed the Court at
great length. He described the prayers and entreaties of
the proprietors of what he termed "this catchpenny
establishment" to induce the grand *Maestro* to lend his
mighty arm and name to their speculation. He had
promised, in writing, to play nowhere but at their
concerts; but as he had played nowhere else, the proprietors could have no legal right to such excessive
damages. The counsel for the plaintiff, Mons. Barillon,
declared that as Paganini's defection had ruined the
speculation, the damages ought to be proportionate to his
transcendent talent. Going into details, he stated that
Paganini was installed in a splendid suite of apartments
at the Casino, one boudoir being lined with flannel
expressly for him; and that when he was complaining of
his wretched health, he accepted a dinner offered him by
the musicians of the orchestra, and gave toasts in both
French and Italian. After that, he allowed bills to be
printed, announcing that he would play at the Casino
concert. Hundreds of tickets were eagerly bought at
twenty francs each, when suddenly Paganini refused to

Plate XI.—See Appendix.

THE HOUSE IN WHICH PAGANINI DIED.

POI CHE DA QVESTA CASA
VOLGENDO IL GIORNO XXVII DI MAGGIO DEL MDCCCXL
LO SPIRITO DI NICOLÒ PAGANINI
SI RICONGIVNSE ALLE FONTI DELLA ETERNA ARMONIA
GIACE L'ARCO POTENTE DI MAGICHE NOTE
MA NELLE AVRE SOAVI DI NIZZA
NE VIVE ANCORA LA DOLCEZZA SVPREMA
C. BONELLI POSE   A. C. BARELLI DETTO
MDCCCLXXXXI

Plate XII.—See Appendix.—TABLET ON HOUSE IN WHICH PAGANINI DIED.

play. Entreaties were in vain; Paganini, in his own room, with closed doors, would practise, but would not play at the concert. Recourse was had to the musicians of the Grand Opera, so as not to disappoint the audience, but the prefect of police would not allow the *employés* of the opera to be taken from their theatre, and ordered the Casino to be closed. Ruin stared the proprietors in the face, and 20,000 francs was no .adequate compensation. The former decision was reversed, and Paganini was condemned by the Court in 50,000 francs* damages, and ten years imprisonment in default of payment.

Whether the fine was actually paid, I have found no evidence to prove, but the imprisonment was certainly not enforced. In a few months' time, the gaoler whom none can deny, touched Paganini with his icy hand, and the troubled spirit left its frail earthly tenement on May 27th, 1840.

But not to rest were the mortal remains consigned. No peaceful grave for the wandering, restless being whose fitful fever of life was over at last. Paganini died without receiving the last Sacrament of the Church. He had indeed been visited by a priest, sent by the Bishop of Nice; but not deeming his end so near, made no confession, nor prepared himself for death according to the rite of the Church of Rome. The doubt as to his faith caused the Bishop of Nice to refuse burial in consecrated ground. The son, the friends of Paganini,

---

* The *Athenæum* puts the amount at 52,000 francs.

and the principal artists of the place solicited the
authorisation of a solemn service for his eternal repose,
but in vain; all that was conceded was the offer of an
authentic record of death, with leave to transport the
corpse whither they might wish. This compromise was
not accepted, and the matter came before the Court of
Justice, when the decision was in favour of the Bishop.
There was no alternative but to appeal to Rome, when
the Bishop's decree was annulled, and the Archbishop of
Turin was charged, conjointly with the Canons of the
Cathedral of Genoa, to institute an inquiry into the
Catholicism of Paganini. Meanwhile the remains—
stated by the *Athenæum* to have been embalmed for
interment at Genoa—were subjected to shocking indignities. The landlord wanted to let the house where the
artist had died, and the corpse was laid in the cellar until
a more fitting resting-place was found. Then it is said
to have been moved to the hospital of Nice, thence by
sea to the *Lazzaretto* of Villa Franca, and finally to a
country house Polcevera, near Genoa, part of the property
of the heir of the illustrious artist. There the body
remained four years. Rumours spread abroad of piteous
moans and other lamentable noises being heard at night.
To put a stop to these unpleasant reports, the young
Baron Achille made an application for permission for a
solemn service to be celebrated at Parma, in virtue of
Paganini having been a knight of St. George. This was
not fruitless. The service was celebrated in the church
of *La Steccata*, appropriated to that order of chivalry.
After the solemnity the friends of the deceased obtained

the permission of the Bishop of Parma to bring the body within the boundary of the Duchy, when it was transferred to the *Villa Gajona*, for interment in the Communal cemetery. So, at last, in May, 1845, the mortal remains of the illustrious violinist were laid in the grave; by order of the government, there was no display of any kind, no outward symbol of homage. The mourners might, however, hope at least for the repose of the casket that once enclosed the fiery, turbulent, soaring spirit of one who knew no rest in life. But, alas! even that was not the end. In the letter addressed by Paganini to the Editor of the Paris *Révue Musicale*, the closing sentence breathed a prayer that, however calumniated he might be in life, the world would at least allow his ashes to repose in peace. That appeal was not granted. It has been shown that five years elapsed between his death and his burial; fifty years more, and the repose of the grave was broken. The *Athenæum* of September 7th, 1895, contained this paragraph :—

" In the Communal Cemetery of Parma the mortal remains of the great violin player, Paganini, have just been exhumed. The violinist was buried there fifty-five years ago, nevertheless his face has been found to be well preserved and easily recognizable. It is proposed to show the body to the public before it is re-interred."

Horrible! But first note the mistake. The body was buried fifty, not fifty-five, years before. Those terrible five years seem to have been unnoticed in this country,

and I have been unable to find any reference to the
mournful function of May, 1845.*

Now, what was the reason for exhuming the remains?
For the purpose of removal to a more prominent site!
Thus is homage paid to genius! Such, too, was the fate
of Beethoven. His remains were removed in 1888 to
the Central Cemetery at Vienna, and lamentable incidents
attended the exhumation. Schubert, who, by his own
desire, was buried by the side of the great master, did
not escape the doom; but Mozart was mercifully spared;
he was buried in a pauper's grave, and his body has
remained undiscovered. The story of the preservation of
his skull may be dismissed as apocryphal. But what are
gorgeous monuments? Does the true artist value the
case more than the instrument? Why seek ye the living
among the dead? The artist does not die—he puts off
the "muddy vesture of decay"; he lives in his art-work.

---

* In the *Musical World* of February 16th, 1843, there is a
paragraph stating that Paganini's remains were still unsepulchred,
the corpse lying in an uninhabited house.

Plate XIII.—See Appendix.

THE TOMB OF PAGANINI AT PARMA.

CHAPTER VIII.

HAVING traced the career of Paganini "from the cradle to the grave," let us now look a little more closely at the man, the artist. Glimpses of his character have already been revealed, but so curiously interesting a personality will repay further study. Totally uneducated, he yet made himself so much a man of the world, as to enjoy the personal friendship of such notabilities as Lord Byron, Sir Thomas Clifford Constable, Lord Holland, Prince Metternich and others. In his official positions at Court he comported himself with dignity. He had the pride of the artist, and would not play if the conditions were not suitable. One instance has already been given. Here is another, which also occurred in Paris. Paganini was asked to play at a Court concert at the Tuilleries. He went the day before to inspect the *salon* where the function was to take place, and found the heavy draperies so numerous that the tones of his violin would be deadened, and the effect of his playing would be lost unless the curtains were removed or rearranged ; he acquainted an official with his wish to alter them. To that august personage a "fiddler" was a mere nobody, and Paganini was given to understand his proper place. Highly offended with the manner of the official, Paganini resolved not to play. The Court was assembled for the concert, but the great violinist was absent. A messenger was sent to his hotel, and was informed that the Signor had retired to rest very early.

Mobbed by ill-mannered crowds whenever he appeared in the streets, (and this especially in London, when strangers not only spoke to him, but even felt him, to ascertain if he was really flesh and blood), Paganini, with his sensitive nature, shrank more and more from contact with the outer world. He was not a Milton, "whose soul was like a star, and dwelt apart," but he was essentially a solitary, a recluse. His character was the result of his environment. Accustomed to brutal treat-ment in his childhood, he became hardened; set free from restraint, he tasted the wild joys of youth, only to find them turn to Dead Sea apples. Schumann, in his "Advice to young musicians." wrote : "The laws of morality are also the laws of art." But Paganini had no mentor, and learnt by bitter experience the lesson of life. He was accused of avarice, and many ridiculous stories were told of him. When at Prague, it is said that even the members of the theatre were struck off the free list, and he was annoyed that the police who watched the upper galleries could not be made to pay for their places ! He beat down a London laundress a halfpenny in her charge for washing his shirts, and Moscheles gives currency to the story, though he cannot vouch for its truth, that Paganini gave his servant a gallery ticket for one of his concerts on condition that the man served him gratuitously for one day ! All these wretched things may have been true, more's the pity. But there is one little story that appears to have been overlooked. The father of Nicolo Paganini was avaricious, and compelled his son to minister to his avarice, even robbing him of the first-fruits of his own earnings; Nicolo in turn became avaricious, but it was for the sake of his little son, whose life he desired might be better than his own. "He saves for his yet uneducated child," wrote Guhr, in 1829. Yes, this man, proud, scornful, despising the crowds whose money made him rich, in the recesses of his heart nourished a love, pure and unselfish. That was the fine gold; his wealth was dross. His affection for the child was boundless, and he allowed the little fellow to tyrannise over him completely. There are pretty stories of his playing with the boy, but there is nothing about teaching the boy to play—the violin. The memory of his own childhood was quite sufficient to deter him from any attempt to force instruction on his boy, and cloud the sunshine of his young life.

The world gave Paganini its plaudits and its money; but there never seemed to be any bond of sympathy between the artist and the public. Yet Paganini could appreciate kindness. Moscheles relates that the father of his wife rendered Paganini some important service before the visit to England. When Paganini first called upon Moscheles he was profuse in expressions of gratitude, and taking down a miniature portrait of his benefactor he covered it with kisses. "Meantime," Moscheles writes, "we had leisure to study those olive-tinted, sharply defined features, the glowing eyes, the scanty, but long black hair, and the thin, gaunt figure, upon which the clothes hung loosely, the deep sunken cheeks, and those long, bony fingers." Moscheles was of service to Paganini during his first days in London, and, to use his own words, he was paid with quite as many honied epithets as his father-in-law received. But he suspected the Italian to be rather too sweet to be genuine. Indeed, the friendship was too fervent to last long, and money was the cause of the rupture. Mori commissioned Moscheles to write a piece " Gems à la Paganini," taking the precaution of obtaining the violinist's consent. His style is imitated, and he expresses his admiration of the piece. A second and third book of " Gems " are published, and down comes Paganini with the charge of musical piracy. His permission extended only to the first book. A lawsuit was commenced, but Paganini effected a compromise with Moscheles, conceding the free sale of the three books of "Gems" in return for pianoforte accompaniments to twelve small violin pieces. Moscheles reluctantly consented to write the accompaniments, but refused to allow his name (which Paganini wanted) to appear on the title-page. Mori had to pay something by way of damages, and Moscheles at last rejoiced at being quit of an episode so little worthy of an artist, and at having done with those dreadful lawyers.*

But quite enough has been said in reference to Paganini's avarice: it has been shown that he had a motive for saving money. Is it as easy to account for

* Life of Moscheles (English Edition), I., p. 252-7.

other traits of his character? That aloofness, that scorn of the world, that hard bargaining: "Take me or leave me," revealing callous indifference, was there no cause for all that? There is a very graphic, and at the same time, appalling, account of the impression produced by Paganini among the Parisians, which is translated at length in Dubourg's "The Violin." Berlioz wrote of the weird genius making his appearance in France during the uproar of the collapse of a dynasty, and arriving in Paris—with the cholera. The terrors of the scourge were powerless to check the tide of curiosity: the people were mad for the time being. This is the conclusion of the notice just mentioned: "Of such a public, and such an artist, how saddening is the sight! . . . . The public, made up of idlers—of beings isolated, cold, corrupt— must be *amused*, forsooth! and the artist exhausts his taste and his sentiment, and well nigh perspires blood and water, to comply with their exactions—to *amuse* them! and if he attain this end, the public clap their hands, the manager of the theatre counts out to him a heap of gold, and he goes away, with his ears deafened at the noise which has surrounded him, and which, for a moment, it may be, has made his heart beat high;—he goes away, with a loving grasp tightened over tbe coin he has so hardly won; and now inwardly exclaims, with a smile of pity, 'The blockheads—the barbarians! who is there among them that can comprehend me—that can *feel* my intentions!' and then the home-returning public, selfish to the very soul, indemnify themselves for their finger's-end applause by sottish contempt, by remarks

that are empty, or worse—that are scornful, bitter,
shocking, disgusting even—such as those which may
have been buzzed into one's ears in Italy or in Paris, but
varied in a hundred ways, and aggravated at will, just as
he varies and enlarges, twists and turns, beneath his
magic bow, a subject of apparently the most simple and
insignificant kind. And now the voices most distinguishable among the ebbing crowd murmur out the words,
' Gambler, Libertine '! or worse. . . . And the privileged
public resort again to the theatre, to admire the talent of
him who they comprehend not ; and the artist returns, in
like manner, to *amuse* those who provoke his pity, and
whom he beholds so far below him ! Thus we have
contempt on one side, compassion on the other ; applause
from hands chilled with the touch of gold, on the one
part,—on the other, sounds that borrow their animation
from no social sympathy ! Such are the relations between
the public and the professor—such the bonds that connect
them ! " Unhappy artist ; miserable public ! How shall
we account for this pitiful state of things, this gulf
between the performer and the auditor ? We must seek
the explanation in the letter to the *Revue*, referred to
more than once, but now claiming our attention more
directly.

The pictures of " Paganini in Prison," exhibited so
lavishly while the artist was in Paris in 1831, provoked
him to remark that there were some " honest. fellows "
making money of a calumny that had pursued his steps
for the last fifteen years. He then referred to the
different versions of the crime imputed to him : that he

Plate XIV.—See Appendix.

PAGANINI IN PRISON.

killed a rival whom he found in company with his mistress; or that it was his mistress who had been the victim of his jealous fury; the only point of agreement was the imprisonment. "Let me tell you," the letter continued, "what happened to myself in Padua about fifteen years ago (1816), on this very subject. I had given a concert with some success: the next day I went to a table-d'hôte; I entered the room late; was, perhaps, the sixtieth guest, and took my seat unnoticed. One of the company expressed himself in flattering terms of the effect produced by my performance the evening before. His next neighbour agreed in the praises bestowed on me, but added, 'Nobody ought to be surprised at Paganini's ability: he owes it all to an eight years' solitary imprisonment in a dungeon, with nothing but his violin to occupy his time, or soften the rigours of his confinement. He was condemned to this long incarceration for having assassinated a friend of *mine*, who was unfortunate enough to be his rival.' As you may easily believe, every one was loud in denouncing the enormity of my crime; when I addressed myself to the speaker, begging him to inform me where and when this tragical adventure had occurred. All eyes were in an instant turned upon me, and you may judge the astonishment of the company at finding the hero of this tale of murder and imprisonment one amongst them. The relater of the story was not a little embarrassed. 'It was not a friend of his own that had fallen—he had heard—he had been told—he believed—but after all it was very possible he might have been deceived,' etc. Now see, Sir, how easy

it is to play with the reputation of an artist merely
because men, inclined to indulge in idleness themselves,
cannot conceive it possible that he may have studied as
closely in his own chamber and in full possession of his
liberty, as he would if he had been chained up in a
dungeon."

There was an occurrence that gave rise to these
reports, and which Paganini related in the same letter.
" A violin player, named D———i,* who was at Milan
in 1798, associated himself with two other men of bad
character, and engaged with them in a plot to assassinate,
by night, the curate of a neighbouring village, supposed
to be in possession of much wealth. Luckily for the
curate the heart of one of the conspirators failed him,
and he denounced his companions. The gendarmes
watched the spot, and took D———i and his accomplice
into custody at the moment they arrived at the curate's
dwelling. They were condemned to twenty years' confinement in irons, but General Menou, after he had been
appointed governor of Milan, at the end of two years
restored the violinist to liberty. Would you believe it,
Sir ? this is the sole foundation upon which the whole
history of my incarceration has been erected. A violin
player, whose name ended in *i*, had been engaged in a
murder and imprisoned—it could only be *Paganini*—the
assassinated party was converted into either my rival or

---

* Duranowski, a talented Polish violinist. He entered the
French army and was *aide-de-camp* to a General. He lost his rank
when released ; returned to his violin, and was living at Strassburg
up to 1834.

my mistress, and it was I, *Paganini*, who had been so
many years loaded with chains, and immured in a
dungeon. Solely with the view of wringing from me the
secret of my new system, have they complimented me
with fetters, whose only effect would have been to
paralyze my arms."

Paganini further stated that he called on the Italian
ambassador resident in Vienna, to testify that he had
known the artist for nearly twenty years, during all
which time his conduct has been that of an honest man.
He also pointed out that having been constantly before
the public from the age of fourteen, he must have had a
mistress and a rival when he was seven! for there was
no room for an interval of eight years afterwards. It
was at Vienna that one of the audience, while Paganini
was playing "The Witches' Dance," distinctly saw the
devil close to the violinist, guiding his fingers and
directing his bow; the said devil was dressed in red and
had horns and a tail, and the striking likeness of the
countenances of the two, plainly proved the relationship
between them. That pretty story followed Paganini
everywhere: and, as has been seen, in Prague he had to
publish a letter from his mother disproving the rumour of
his Satanic parentage. There is something intensely
pathetic in Paganini's conclusion: "I see nothing else
for it but to leave malignity at liberty to disport itself at
my expense."

In this prosaic, materialistic twentieth century, which
believes in little besides money, there is no fear of any of
our violin wonders being associated with the arch-fiend.

They may be regarded as physic problems, but the
supernatural is eliminated from the study. But Paganini
did not live in the twentieth century, and in his day the
devil was a very real personage, notwithstanding the
temporary overthrow of much belief through the French
Revolution, and the enthronement of the " Goddess of
Reason" in the Church of Notre Dame, Paris. It may
seem absurd, now, even to recall these calumnies ; but
we have to deal with the environment of a great genius,
to study the cause of his failing to become great as a
man ; for surely he had the making of a fine character.
That he should traverse the greater part of Europe,
pursued by tales of devilry and murder, is one of
the saddest comments on that period ; that the " iron
entered into his soul," and the man capable of
affection became a miser and a misanthrope, is more
mournful still. He was the " Flying Dutchman " of
the violin.

How was it that the devil and the violin came into
relationship? We have it on the authority of Martin
Luther that the devil hates music. Luther not only
believed in the devil, but he fancied he saw him : and in
the room of the Castle of Wartburg may still be seen the
mark on the wall, where he threw his inkpot at the fiend,
who tried to thwart his work of translating the Bible. It
is curious that the only instrument which, to the present
writer's knowledge, Satan has been represented as playing upon, is one of the precursors of the violin. There is
a piece of sculpture in the Cathedral of Amiens, depicting
Satan playing on an oval three-stringed Vielle, of the

thirteenth century.* The story of Tartini and his dream, when the devil played so marvellously on the violin, is known to everyone, and is, moreover, perpetuated in the sonata *Il Trillo del Diavolo.* It is related of Thomas Baltzar, the first great violinist ever heard in England, that when he played at Oxford he astonished everyone by " running up his fingers to the end of the finger-board." John Wilson, the Oxford Professor of Music, " the greatest judge of musick that ever was," according to Anthony à Wood, " did, after his humoursome way, stoop down to Baltzar's feet, to see whether he had a huff on, that is to say, whether he was a devil or not, because he acted beyond the parts of man." As this took place in 1658 there was some excuse for the grim pleasantry ; moreover music had suffered an eclipse, and performers in this country were comparatively few. Even the gentle and polite Corelli forgot himself so far as to apply the term, devil, to another violinist. As the story may not be so well known as the foregoing, I shall briefly repeat it. Nicolaus Adam Strungk (or Strunck), violinist to Ernest Augustus, Elector of Hanover, when in Rome (*circa* 1684) made it his business to see Corelli. Introducing himself to the Italian master as a musician, Corelli asked what was his instrument. Strungk replied that he could play upon the harpsichord, and a little upon the violin ; but he particularly wished to hear Corelli on the latter instrument, his fame being widely known. Corelli obligingly consented, and played a piece to the

* An engraving of it is in Naumann's "History of Music" (English Edition), p. 255.

harpsichord accompaniment of Strungk. Strungk afterwards played a toccata, with which Corelli was so much
taken that he laid aside his instrument in his transport of
admiration. When Strungk had finished at the harpsichord, he took up the violin, and began handling it in a
careless manner, whereupon Corelli remarked that he had
a good bow-hand, and wanted nothing but practice to
become a master of his instrument. At that moment
Strungk put the violin out of tune, and played on with
such dexterity, attempering the dissonances occasioned
by the mistuning with such amazing skill, that Corelli
cried out in broken German : " I am called Arcangelo, a
name that in the language of my country signifies an
Archangel ; but let me tell you, that you, Sir, are an
Arch-devil ! "

There is nothing malicious in these stories of the devil
and the fiddler ; and if Paganini had experienced nothing
worse than what has just been related, he might have
treated the matter as a joke. But that which malice or
envy originated, a "reptile press" promulgated. Innocent
of crime, Paganini was branded as a felon ; gifted with
genius of the rarest order, cultivated to a perfection
absolutely unique, his skill was attributed to the aid
received from the devil. Add to this his wretched health,
and there is both mental and bodily suffering. In his
later years he was cut off from intercourse with others,
like Beethoven—but with this difference : Beethoven
employed a tablet or note-book for his friends to convey
their words to him ; Paganini transmitted, through a
similar medium, his thoughts to others. He was dumb !

Is there no brighter side to this picture ? If there be, let us turn to it.

It is, perhaps, fortunate that no man can be consistent throughout his life; the morose must smile at times, and the misanthrope mitigate his hatred of mankind. Paganini was but human, and his life was not all shadow. Though his intimate friends were few, there were some who were able to place on record details of the private life of the great violinist. Of such, the most useful to biographers was George Harris. He was an Englishman, attached to the Court at Hanover—then connected with Britain; a dramatist of a certain order, he accompanied Paganini on his tours in Germany, acting for a time as his secretary, and apparently he was with him when in England. From him we learn a good deal.

Paganini was always on the move, and travelling in his day was not the rapid, comfortable, even luxurious process it is now. In the post-chaise Paganini stowed his luggage, which was of the simplest—and shabbiest— description. A dilapidated box held his beloved violin, his linen, cash and jewellery; a carpet-bag and a hat-box completed his outfit. He was philosophically indifferent to comfort, but in his later years he always had the windows of his carriage closed. When he arrived at his quarters, the windows of his room were thrown open, and he indulged in a sun-bath—again anticipating modern medical advice. Paganini, when travelling, was fond of taking a stroll when the horses were changed. It was a relief to stretch his legs after the close confinement of the post-chaise, but sometimes his rambles were so

prolonged that there was weary waiting for him when all
was ready to resume the journey, and drivers became
exasperated. Paganini was made to suffer on one
occasion. That was when travelling from London to
Birmingham. He had already tried the patience of his
coachman by causing loss of time, and the man declared
he would drive on without him, rather than wait again.
At the next stopping place Paganini walked off as usual,
leaving Harris asleep in the vehicle. The horses being
changed, the driver started, leaving Paganini behind.
This caused some trouble, for a post-chaise had to be
sent from the next station in search of the derelict, and
Paganini in his rage refused to pay the extra expense.
He was summoned before the Birmingham magistrates,
and the case going against him he was compelled to
discharge the debt. Poor Paganini, he always suffered
when he came into contact with the law.

In his personal habits Paganini was simplicity itself.
Frugal to a degree in his repasts, a cup of chocolate
sufficed for a meal when starting early on a journey, and
often he would fast until evening. When in a happy
mood after a concert, he would join the table d'hôte and
do as others did, but the slightest indulgence was
punished the next day. He preferred solitude, but when
he mixed with others he would join freely in the conversation; if music were touched upon he became silent,
or left the room. So long as he could find accommodation
that was quiet, he cared little for its quality. Scenery
had no charms for him, and all climates but his own
were equally indifferent to him. His accounts were kept

in a little red pocket-book (found under his pillow after
his death), in a kind of arithmetical shorthand only
decipherable by himself.   He never had been taught the
science of numbers, or he might have been made a first-
rate mathematician.

Harris stated that all the time he was with Paganini
he never heard him play a single note except before an
audience.   That may have been correct so far as
Germany was concerned, but the Rev. John Edmund
Cox, in his "Musical Recollections," has something very
different to say about Paganini.   "During his career he
visited my native town,"* and as I had the good fortune
then to be able to converse in French, the friends who
had engaged him for a round of concerts in that place
and its vicinity placed me in direct communication with
him somewhat in the capacity of a secretary; so that I
not only travelled in his company and heard him at every
concert at which he appeared, but I lived in the same
hotels and lodgings which had been secured for him.
This kind of semi-official position necessitated my seeing
much of him during his leisure hours, when he threw off
the suspicious restraint which was always apparent in his
manner when he was among strangers, whom he
imagined were bent upon getting as much as possible out
of him for their own advantage.   Then, indeed, he would
evince anything but a hard and ungenerous nature, his
manner being not only kind but courteous; whilst any
attention that was afforded to his wants or to his comforts

---

* Norwich.

was sure to elicit not only looks but words of gratitude. In public he confined himself almost exclusively to the performance of his own music,—. . . but in private—for he had his violin constantly in his hand—he would sit and dash off by the hour together snatches from the compositions of the best masters, and give readings of such originality to passages that had been heard again and again, as apparently have never been supposed to be possible by any other player. As an instance in point, he one morning, whilst I was writing several notes for him, commenced the first *motivo* of Beethoven's magnificent violin concerto. To write was then impossible; and he, perceiving how entranced I seemed, asked whether I knew what it was. On my replying in the negative, he promised, if it could be managed, that I should hear the whole of that movement before we separated." The promise was redeemed. The above is valuable as show- ing that Paganini was not quite so wanting in knowledge as was generally supposed. He could converse in French, though at that time—1831—he had only spent a few weeks in France. Education, proper, he had none; but the statement that he could speak no language but his own, is evidently incorrect. The allusion to strangers bent upon getting as much as possible out of him for their own advantage, finds an illustration in the story of the Englishman who is said to have followed Paganini for some six months, watching his every movement, lodging at the same hotels, and employing every means to get at the great secret of the violinist's art. At last his perseverance seemed about to be rewarded. Looking

Monsieur

Je vous témoigne toute ma satisfaction pour le soin que vous avez bien voulu donner pour mon cher fils Achille. J'y joins mes vœux pour que vous puissiez exercer vos connaissance afin de pouvoir par là améliorer votre sort, auquel je m'intéresse beaucoup

J'ai l'avantage de vous saluer avec considération

Nicolò Paganini.

Paris 16 avril 1832

PLATE 15. (*See Appendix.*)

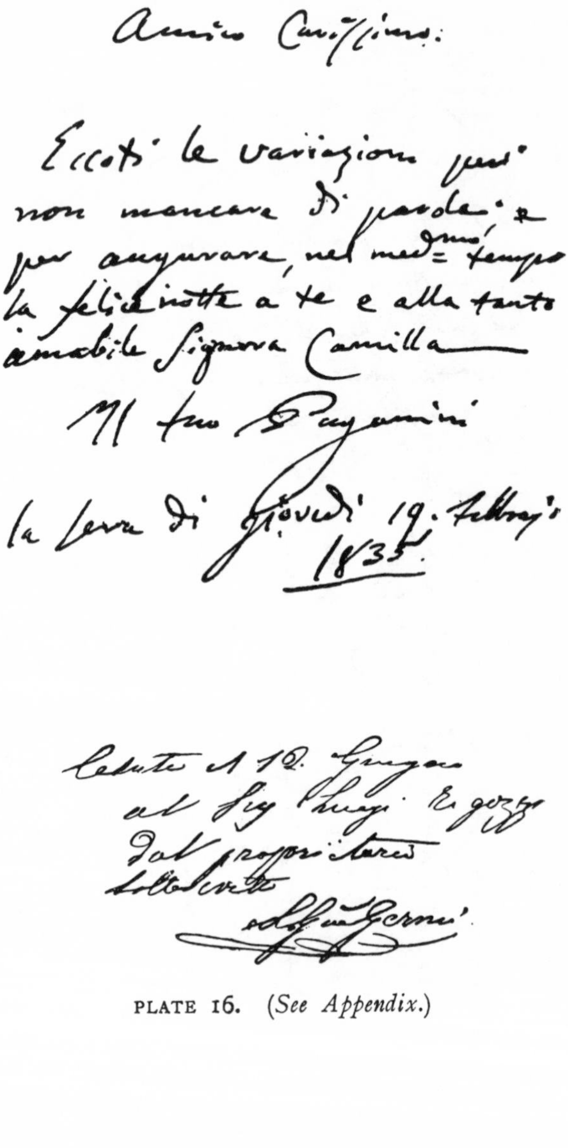

Amico Carissimo:

Eccoti le variazioni per
non mancare di parole; e
per augurare, nel med.mo tempo
la felice notte a te e alla tanto
amabile Signora Camilla ——
      Il tuo Paganini

la Sera di Giovedì 19. Febbraio
                    1835.

ceduta il 12. Giugno
al Sig Luigi Ri gozzi
dal proprietario
sottoscritto
            adolfo Germi

PLATE 16. (See Appendix.)

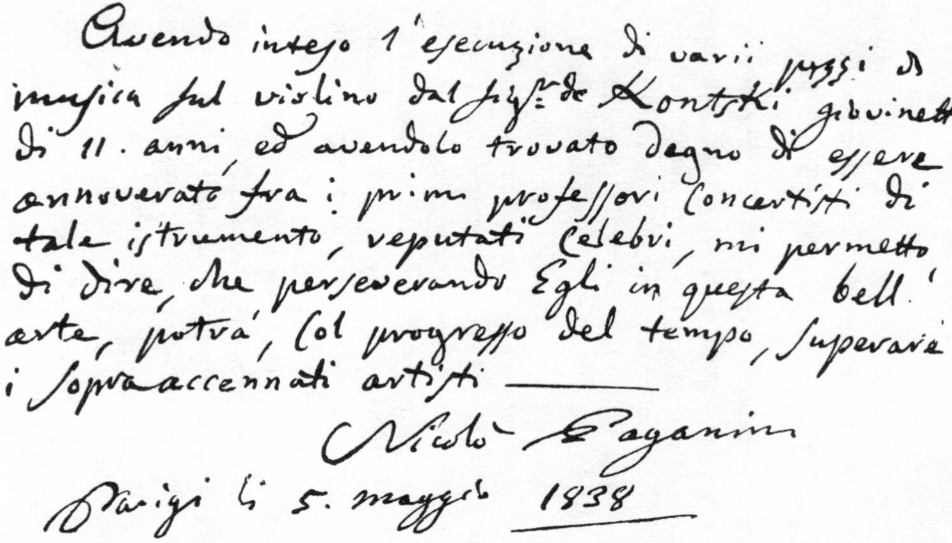

Avendo inteso l'esecuzione di varii pezzi di
musica del violino dal Sig:re Kontski giovinetto
di 11. anni, ed avendolo trovato degno di essere
annoverato fra i primi professori concertisti di
tale istromento, reputati celebri, mi permetto
di dire, che perseverando Egli in questa bell'
arte, potrà (col progresso del tempo) superare
i sopraccennati artisti. —————

Nicolò Paganini

Parigi li 5. maggio 1838
—————

PLATE 17. (*See Appendix.*)

through the keyhole of Paganini's door, the Englishman
saw the violinist take his instrument from its case—raise
it to his shoulder, even shift the left hand up and down
the neck; but not the ghost of a sound. It was just
a study of positions, and the violin was then restored to
its place. In despair, the inquisitive amateur gave up
the quest.

The concerts Paganini gave for the poor were evidence
of his natural goodness of heart. It is true, such efforts
cost him little; he gave a few hours' time: the public
found the money. One day, when walking in Vienna, he
saw a poor little Italian boy playing the violin in front of
a large house. He drew from him a touching story of
poverty, and a sick mother; and emptying his pockets
into the boy's hands, he took from him his violin and
began to play. He was soon recognised, and a crowd
assembled; the people were immensely diverted, and
gave a generous response when the hat was handed
round. With " Take that to your mother," Paganini
sent the boy off rejoicing, and turning to the companion
of his walk, he remarked, " I hope I've done a good turn
to that little animal." He was fond of applying the word
" animal" to those sometimes spoken of as " the lower
classes," but was not altogether singular in that respect.

At the anniversary dinner of the Royal Society of
Musicians, in 1832, among the donations announced was
one of ten guineas from Paganini. This was thought so
excessively mean an acknowledgment of the generosity
of the English nation, that the announcement was
received with groans and hisses. That was distinctly

rude on the part of those who, having dined well, ought
to have been in a genial state of mind.

At least one generous action must be placed on record.
It was told by George Augustus Sala many years ago.*
The mother of that voluminous writer was a vocalist,
and made her *début* at Covent Garden Theatre in 1827,
as the Countess in Bishop's version (or perversion) of
Mozart's "Marriage of Figaro." In 1828 she became a
widow, and supported her family by teaching singing and
giving annual concerts, chiefly at Brighton, where she
lived. For one of her benefit concerts she engaged
Paganini. The most distinguished artists of her day had
gladly given their gratuitous assistance at similar
functions, and Paganini accepted the small fee of twenty-
five guineas. Sala was a very small boy at that time
(born in 1828), and possibly drew upon his imagination
when recounting the event so many years later. This is
what he wrote:—"'Take your little boy with you,
Madame Sala,' was the shrewd counsel of ———, a
valued friend of my mother; 'take the boy with you
when you pay Pag.; perhaps *that* will soften him a little.'
I was the smallest and chubbiest of the tribe; then, duly
washed, combed and made spruce, my parent took me in
her hand, and led me to the Old Ship, where Paganini
was staying. We were ushered, not without fear and
trembling on my part, into the presence of the mighty
musician, who was at breakfast. Then my mother,
alluding as far as she in delicacy could to her large family

---

* In the "Bow Bells Annual" for 1878 (?)

and small means, proceeded to count out—sovereign by
sovereign, shilling by shilling—Paganini's fee of five and
twenty guineas. I can see with the eye of memory the
whole man before me now, his gaunt angular form, his
black elf-like locks falling in weird confusion over his
neck and shoulders, his cadaverous face and shaggy
brows, his long bony hands with the veins standing out
like cordage, his amazingly large feet, and especially his
neck, disproportionately long, scraggy, and corrugated.
I can see the glare—so it seemed to me—which, when he
raised his bent brows, darted upon the pile of money, and
the spasmodic avidity with which he extended his hand
and swept the pile towards him. . . . . 'A very nice little
boy,' he was good enough to say, alluding to myself; 'but
time is bad, and there is no monish in de vorld : no, never
no monish at all.' My mother rose with a heavy heart to
depart. 'Stop, little boy,' said the great violinist, and he
beckoned to me with a skinny finger, which any of the
witches in Macbeth would have been proud to own ;
'stop, take this, it will buy you a cake.' He thrust a
crumpled piece of paper into my hand, rose from his
chair, and, without more ado 'bolted'—that is the only
word suited to the action—into his bedroom. He had
given me a bank note for fifty pounds! Superstitious
people used to whisper that Paganini had sold himself to
the enemy of mankind ; spiteful people used to draw him
as a greedy, flint-hearted miser. . . . . I only know how
he acted towards my mother."

CHAPTER IX.

FROM the man we now turn to the artist. Schiller wrote: "The artist is the son of his age, but pity for him if he is its pupil or even its favourite." It has been shown how truly Paganini was the child of his age; the pity was that he became its pupil and its favourite; in consequence he failed to attain the supreme height where dwell the spirits of the greatest. But he was a great artist, in spite of his concessions to the public taste; and he held in reverence that which he found great in others. When in Vienna in 1828, exactly a year after the death of Beethoven, Paganini attended a concert, and heard a performance of the great master's Symphony, No. 7, in A. Profoundly moved by that sublime composition, he remained mute, his gaze fixed and mournful; suddenly the tears rolled from his eyes; his grief and emotion wrung from him the words: *E morto!* Anders, who relates the incident, adds: "Never was the immortal author of *Fidelio* more worthily extolled than by those tears, by that simple word. The day may come when some disciple, some friend of the Genoese artist, will say in his turn, seized with bitter sadness, *E morto!*" Strange, that Chorley should have employed the very words, in the premature obituary notice which has been already referred to.

When in Paris, Paganini once visited the Institution for the Blind. He was so much struck with the beauty and purity of intonation that characterised the singing of the pupils, that he declared that never before had he an adequate notion of what harmony was.

The artist, as well as the art, claimed his respect. There seems to have been no artistic jealousy about him, and to the young performer he was invariably kind, whilst to the established professor he was just. It is said that when Paganini's concerts took place at the King's Theatre, it was proposed to dispense with the services of the "leader" at the Opera. When Paganini heard of this, he paid a well-merited compliment to the abilities of Signor Spagnoletti, and insisted upon his engagement at all the concerts, he, Paganini, might give at the Theatre. It is true, at rehearsal, Paganini never gratified the members of the orchestra as to what the concert performances were likely to be ; but he was careful to have the accompaniments well prepared.   Quick-tempered, he was irritated at any faulty work, but when all went well he expressed his approbation by exclaiming, "*Bravissimi !* *Siete tutti virtuosi !* " (" You are all artists ! ") Paganini brought the orchestral parts with him to rehearsal, and took them away afterwards ; as to the solo part, no one had a chance of looking at that, for Paganini played everything from memory.   His kindness to brother-artists has been placed on record.   The young violon-cellist Ciandelli, who rendered such service to Paganini when he was turned into the street by the brutal landlord, was afterwards well repaid by the instruction Paganini gave him. The great violinist told Schottky, his biographer, that he took a lively interest in young Ciandelli, and that he imparted to him his secret. He gave him lessons, and at the end of three days so transformed his playing, that from being a mediocre performer, he became the first violoncellist at the Theatre Royal, Naples, with a possibility of becoming the first in the world. However, as history is silent respecting the subsequent achievements of Gaetano Ciandelli, he need not claim further attention.

The Bohemian violinist, Joseph Slavik, appeared at Vienna in 1826, when he was twenty years of age. Moscheles heard him play, and said he was considered in Vienna as the second Paganini. Of course that was hearsay; *the* Paganini had not then been heard outside Italy. When Paganini was in Vienna, in 1828, he become acquainted with young Slavik, and held him in affectionate regard. At all hours the young student had access to the idol of his worship, and received many valuable hints and ideas upon fingering, etc., and friendly encouragement to pursue his daring course with unwearying application. He spent two years in retirement, zealously studying the Paganini method, and when he reappeared in Vienna, he was spoken of as no petty imitator, but a second original. A contemporary notice, comparing Slavik with Paganini, states:—" The only difference between the two at present is, that the pupil, carried away by the ardour of youth, often suffers himself

to be seduced into the most gigantic attempts, the success
of which on every occasion no mortal can with certainty
rely upon; while the other, possessing the plaintive and
deeply pathetic tones of a singer, at the same time
resembles a consummate piece of musical mechanism,
which accomplishes the most extraordinary feats quietly
and without effort." Slavik died at Pesth, in 1833, at the
early age of twenty-seven; what he might have become
his actual achievements plainly indicated.

In his later years, Paganini appears to have had great
delight in listening to young artists. In 1836, Antonio
Bazzini, then a youth of eighteen, played to Paganini,
who was enraptured with his performance. A year later,
in Paris, Paganini heard a much younger violinist, the
boy Apollinaire de Kontski, and actually went so far as
to give him a testimonial. Articles in the musical
dictionaries all state that Paganini gave some lessons to
the child; some say that the friendship between the two
resulted in Paganini bequeathing to De Kontski his
violins and compositions. Grove, in quoting Mendel,
says this statement requires confirmation. When Apollinaire de Kontski died, in 1879, nothing, so far as I have
been able to ascertain, transpired concerning the alleged
bequest. But the testimonial seems to have escaped the
notice of dictionary compilers, so, as a curiosity, I
reproduce it from the *Musical World*, of June 21st,
1838:—

"Having heard M. de Kontski, aged eleven years,
perform several pieces of music on the violin, and having
found him worthy of being ranked among the most

celebrated artists of the present day, permit me to say, that if he continues his studies in this fine art, he will, in course of time, surpass the most distinguished performers of the age.   (Signed)   PAGANINI."

But if Paganini was fond of hearing and encouraging other artists, he was averse to anything like competitive display. When he met Lafont at Milan in 1816, as already related, he played at the concert given by that artist. The function came to be regarded as a contest, and an account of it appears in Laphaléque's pamphlet. Some paper, early in 1830, having quoted this notice, Lafont wrote a letter of protest, which is interesting enough to reproduce in part. He wrote:—

"Sir, I have just read, in your journal of the 2nd of Feb., an extract from the Notice published on the celebrated violinist, Paganini. As this notice contains statements utterly erroneous, as regards me, I owe it to truth, to the advice of my friends, and to the favour with which the public has been pleased to honour me during twenty-five years, to give an exact statement of the facts of the case. The following is a narration of what occurred. In the month of March, 1816, I gave in conjunction with M. Paganini, a concert in the great theatre, La Scala, at Milan, and, far from making a cruel trial of the powers of my adversary, or of being beaten by him, as is pretended by the author of the Notice, I obtained a success the more flattering, as I was a stranger in the country and had no other support than my talent.

"I played, with M. Paganini, the concerted symphony

of Kreutzer, in *fa* major.   For several days previously to
the concert we rehearsed this symphony together, and
with the greatest care.   On the day of the concert it was
performed by us as it had been rehearsed, with no change
whatever; and we both obtained an equal success in the
passages executed together or separately.   On coming to
the *phrase de chant* in *fa* minor, in the second solo of the
first part, there was a decided advantage for one of us.
This passage is of a deep and melancholy expression.
M. Paganini performed it first.   Whether the strong and
pathetic character of the piece was ill-suited to the
ornaments and brilliant notes which he gave in it, or
whatever else was the cause, his *solo* produced but little
effect.   Immediately after him, I repeated the same
passage, and treated it differently.   It seems that the
emotion by which I was then agitated, caused me to give
an expression more effective, though more simple, and it
was so felt by the audience, that I was overwhelmed
with plaudits from all parts of the house.   During
fourteen years I have been silent on this trifling advantage
obtained over M. Paganini in this instance, only in the
symphony, and probably rather by the superiority of the
school than by that of talent.   It is painful to me to
speak of myself ; nothing short of the misrepresentation
of the article in question could have provoked me to
reply.   I was not beaten by M. Paganini, nor was he by
me.   On all occasions, I have taken pleasure in rendering
homage to his great talent ; but I have never said that he
was the first violinist in the world ; I have not done such
injustice to the celebrated men—Kreutzer, Rode, Baillot,

and Habeneck, and I declare now, as I have always done, that the French school is the first in the world for the violin."

After this modest assertion Lafont concludes with an expression of rejoicing in the opportunity of praising a talent of which he felt it an honour to be the rival, but of which no one could make him the adversary.

This epistle provoked a rejoinder from Francesco Cianchettini* who wrote:—"As I was present at that contest, I do assert that the account given by Mr. Imbert is not erroneous, but correct. The public decision was in favour of Paganini; Mr. Lafont having acquiesced in silence to such a decision, does not diminish one iota of his acquired fame: as not only himself, but every living violinist who dares to enter into rivalry with Paganini, will be prostrated, although the Signor has not had the advantage of being a pupil of the *super-excellent Parisian Violin School.* In Paris, I have heard how the talented violinists, mentioned in Mr. Lafont's letter, speak of Paganini. The *Coriosi* gladiators of the Neronian age spoke with the same freedom of Hercules. Had this demigod suddenly appeared on the arena with his club, all of them would instantly have shrunk into pigmies."

In a footnote Cianchettini added that whatever excellence the Parisian Violin School might lay claim to, was derived from Italians; from Viotti, through Pugnani and Tartini, to Corelli, "the father of the violin."

---

* Little is now known of this artist. He married Veronica, sister of the pianist and composer J. L. Dussek, and was the father of Pio Cianchettini, composer, who died at Cheltenham in 1851.

But the genius of Paganini was fully understood and appreciated by a far greater Frenchman than Charles Lafont:—Hector Berlioz.

The friendship between Paganini and Berlioz has been briefly referred to, but it is a subject for further consideration, as it reveals the influence that the one artist wielded over the other. The first meeting of the two men must be told in the words of Berlioz himself. A few remarks are needed by way of preface. In the summer of 1833, Berlioz married the English actress Miss Smithson, who, still weak from her carriage accident, had, on her wedding day, "nothing in the world but debts, and the fear of never again being able to appear to advantage on the stage." To pay off these debts Berlioz organized a benefit entertainment, beginning with drama and ending with a concert. But his programme was too long, and he had forgotten something—*the claque*. His poor wife could not conceal her lameness, and though talented as ever, she failed to obtain a recall. Another actress, having taken precautions, had an ovation. Then at midnight the band of the *Théâtre Italien*, not being obliged to play after that hour, left the place, and the *Symphonie Fantastique* could not be played. Liszt assisted, and the affair was not quite a failure, financially, though the promoter came in for bitter attacks. Poor Berlioz was in despair, but he took his courage in both hands, and announced a concert at the *Conservatoire*. He took care to engage artists he could trust, and with his friend Girard as conductor everything went well, the *Symphonie Fantastique* taking the room by storm. Now let Berlioz speak: " My success was complete, and the former judgment on me was reversed. My musicians looked radiant with delight as they left the orchestra. Lastly, my happiness was completed when the public had all gone, and a man stopped me in the passage—a man with long hair, piercing eyes, a strange and haggard face—a genius, a Titan among the giants, whom I had never seen before, and at first sight of whom I was deeply moved ; this man pressed my hand, and overwhelmed me with burning eulogies, which literally set both my heart and brain on fire. It *was Paganini* (22nd December, 1833). From that date my relations with that great artist, who exercised such a happy influence upon my destiny, and whose noble generosity has given birth to such absurd and malicious comments."

It was some time in January, 1834, that Paganini called upon Berlioz and said he had a wonderful viola, a Stradivari, upon which he should much like to play in public, but he had no music for it. Would Berlioz write a solo for him ? Berlioz was flattered by the proposal, but replied that in order to produce a composition sufficiently brilliant to suit such a virtuoso, he—Berlioz —ought to be able to play the viola, and that he could not do. So he thought Paganini alone could meet his own wishes. Paganini, however, pressed his own point, adding that he himself was too unwell to compose anything. Berlioz then set to work. To quote his own words: "In order to please the illustrious virtuoso, I then endeavoured to write a solo for the viola, but so combined with the orchestra as not to diminish the importance of the latter, feeling sure that Paganini's incomparable execution would enable him to give the solo instrument all its due prominence. The proposition was a new one. A happy idea soon occurred to me, and I became intensely eager to carry it out."

Paganini was impatient to see the music, and as soon as the first movement was finished, it was shown to him. He did not like the long silences. "That is not at all what I want," he said; "I must be playing the whole time." "You really want a *concerto* for the tenor," Berlioz replied, "and you are the only man who can write it." Paganini said no more, and soon afterwards left for Nice. Berlioz then gave free play to his fancy, and wrote the series of scenes for the orchestra, the background formed from the recollections of his wanderings in the Abruzzi, the viola introduced as a sort of melancholy dreamer, in the style of Byron's "Childe Harold." Hence the title "Harold in Italy." Now, this is the point: "Harold" was inspired by Paganini, who indirectly gave a new art-form to the world. The piece was produced on November 23rd, 1834, but Paganini was then in Italy, and he did not hear it until four years later.

But Paganini was destined to inspire something greater still. He was again in Paris in 1838, and, as before related, was present at the "horrible performance" of Berlioz' "Benvenuto Cellini." Sad at heart Paganini said: "If I were manager of the *Opéra*, I would at once engage that young man* to write me three such operas:

---

* Berlioz was then thirty-five, Paganini, fifty-six years of age.

I would pay him in advance, and should make a capital bargain by it." The failure of the opera threw Berlioz on a bed of sickness. But he had to live, and was soon arranging to give concerts at the *Conservatoire*. The first barely paid expenses, but the second, at which both the *Symphonie Fantastique* and *Harold en Italie* were performed, was more successful, and at this Paganini was present. This has also been incidentally mentioned, but further notice is required on account of the sequel. Again we must allow Berlioz to speak for himself. " The concert was just over; I was in a profuse perspiration, and trembling with exhaustion, when Paganini, followed by his son Achilles, came up to me at the orchestra door, gesticulating violently. Owing to the throat affection of which he ultimately died, he had already completely lost his voice, and unless everything was perfectly quiet, no one but his son could hear or even guess what he was saying. He made a sign to the child, who got up on a chair, put his ear close to his father's mouth and listened attentively. Achilles then got down, and turning to me, said, ' My father desires me to assure you, sir, that he has never in his life been so powerfully impressed at a concert; that your music has quite upset him, and that if he did not restrain himself he should go down on his knees to thank you for it.' I made a movement of incredulous embarrassment at these strange words, but Paganini seizing my arm, and rattling out ' Yes, yes!' with the little voice he had left, dragged me up on the stage, where there were still a good many of the performers, knelt down, and kissed my hand. I need not describe my stupefaction; I relate the facts, that is all."

In his frenzied state Berlioz went out into the bitter cold, met Armand Bertin on the boulevard, told him what had occurred, caught a chill, and again had to keep his bed. Two days later, the little Achilles called, the bearer of a letter, and of a message to the effect that his father would himself have paid the visit, but was too ill to do so. The letter ran as follows:—

"My Dear Friend,

Beethoven dead, only Berlioz now can revive him; and I, who have enjoyed your divine compositions, worthy of the genius which you are, entreat you to accept, in token of my homage, twenty thousand francs, which will be remitted you by the Baron de Rothschild on presentation of the enclosed. Believe me always your most affectionate friend,   Nicolo Paganini.

Paris, December 18th, 1838."

Picture the scene! Berlioz, pale with excitement; his wife, entering the room, imagines some new misfortune has befallen them. Told of what has happened, she calls her son Louis. Berlioz' words again: "And my wife and child ran back together, and fell on their knees beside my bed, the mother praying, the child in astonishment joining his little hands beside her. O Paganini! what a sight! Would that he could have seen it!"

The news soon spread abroad, and there were mixed feelings with regard to Berlioz; delight on the one hand, detractions on the other, and "scandalous insinuations" against Paganini. It was some six days before Berlioz recovered sufficiently to visit and thank Paganini. The latter would not hear a word; it was the greatest pleasure he had ever felt in his life, he said; adding, " Ah! now none of the people who cabal against you will dare to say another word, for they know that I am a good judge, and that I am not easy " the last clause bearing two meanings: " I am not in easy circumstances," or, " I do not part with money easily." I know that this gift of Paganini to Berlioz is now regarded as a myth. One version of the story is that Paganini was merely the agent, the real donor being Armand Bertin, the great friend of Berlioz, who wished to remain in the background. Another version is to the effect that Jules Janin, editor of the *Journal des Débats*, compelled Paganini to make the gift to Berlioz, who was the musical critic on that paper; and that Paganini, fearing to lose his prestige with the public if Berlioz turned against him, yielded to the pressure put upon him. I am going to give chapter and verse for all this, for it is a matter that should be put at rest. But first, what a condition is revealed of the press in relation to art. Berlioz in money matters was incorruptable, though he was often poor enough; therefore I leave him out of the discussion. But think of the possibility of the transaction! Janin, years before, had written bitter things of Paganini— things I have declined to quote in this memoir; but Janin must have been quite as bad as he asserted Paganini to have been, if he was capable of this

monstrous proposition. There are two details to be
considered, and the first is the date. In 1838, the public
career of Paganini was at an end. There was the
wretched Casino business, it is true, but there was no
performance by Paganini. In the second place, supposing
for a moment that Berlioz could or would employ his pen
in disparagement of the great violinist, could he have
written anything more violent, more depreciatory, than
critics had been writing for the previous twenty years,
criticisms which Paganini had survived, and grown rich
upon? Besides, if the Janin story be true, the Bertin
must be false. Where then is the authority for the
former? In 1840, Liszt wrote a memorial notice of
Paganini. In it passing reference is made to some deeds
of benevolence. Lina Ramann, in her " Life of Liszt,"
of which the first part was published in 1880, prints this
essay, and at the point above mentioned adds a long foot
note* giving the Janin story, which she averred Liszt
knew through Janin himself. That was a safe story to
reproduce, though it might have been contradicted by
Liszt if he ever saw the book. Now for the Bertin
version. The authority quoted for that is always
Ferdinand Hiller. In 1868, Hiller published his work
" On the Musical Life of our Time," in which he relates
some gossiping with Rossini, in 1856. The conversation
turned upon Paganini on one occasion, and Hiller asked
about the kingly gift to Berlioz. Rossini replied that all
Paris knew it, and he must needs believe it, but at
bottom he held the thing impossible. Nothing more

---

* Aus dem Tonleben unserer Zeit, Vol. II., p. 55.

definite is there recorded. In 1871, Hiller published a
new series of similar papers or essays, but of this work I
know nothing. Rossini was a raconteur, and fond of
saying good things. There is no reason to doubt the
good faith of Ferdinand Hiller; he set down what Rossini
said, which, after all, was only the expression of a doubt.
This reticence was perhaps owing to the fact that Berlioz
was still living. But how was Rossini likely to know the
facts of the case? He went to Italy in 1836, and
returned to Paris about the end of May, 1855; conse-
quently he knew nothing of the alleged gift at the time,
and as Armand Bertin died in 1854, Rossini could not
have heard the story from him. So far, one would be
justified in attaching little credence to Hiller's gossip
with Rossini.

But there was a sequel. Rossini died in November,
1868, and Berlioz passed away in March, 1869. His
Autobiography was published in 1870, with the Paganini
incident as it has already been related. To the last,
Berlioz believed that the money came from Paganini.
In 1880, Hiller published a work entitled "Künstlerleben,"
in which a chapter was devoted to Berlioz. Again
reference is made to the princely gift, incredible from so
mean a man as Paganini. "Rossini gave me the key to
this enigma," writes Hiller, "and I do not hesitate to
communicate the same, as it can no longer be unpleasant
to anyone concerned in the matter." He then goes on
to say that Paganini consented to be the agent of Armand
Bertin, who really found the money. "Are you sure
that this was true?" asked Hiller; "I *know* it," replied

Rossini, seriously. Hiller then states his conviction that Rossini's account must be correct.* Now was this the outcome of a subsequent conversation with Rossini, or an amplification of the "gossip" at Trouville? Hiller is candid enough to say that some may doubt, and I should confess to being among the doubters if his evidence was the sole support of the story.

But in 1896, appeared the evidence of one whose testimony was unimpeachable. The late Sir Charles Hallé went to Paris in 1836, when a youth of seventeen. In 1838, he was introduced to Paganini, was invited to visit him, and often played to him; and, once, nearly heard Paganini play! An extract from Hallé's "Autobiography" will show what he thought of the great violinist: "From my earliest childhood I had heard of Paganini and his art as of something supernatural, and there I actually sat opposite to the man himself, but only looking at the hands that had created such wonders. On one never-to-be-forgotten occasion, after I had played and we had enjoyed a long silence, Paganini rose and approached his violin case. What then passed in me can hardly be imagined; I was all in a tremble, and my heart thumped as if it would burst my chest; in fact, no young swain going to the first rendezvous with his beloved could possible feel more violent emotions. Paganini opened the case, took the violin out, and began to tune it carefully with his fingers without using the bow; my agitation became almost intolerable. When he was satisfied, and I said to myself, with a lump in my throat,

---

* Künstlerleben, p. 88.

'Now, now, he'll take the bow!' he carefully put the
violin back and shut the case. And this is how I heard
Paganini." Hailé also became acquainted with Berlioz
and acquaintance ripened into a close friendship. He
saw the change worked in Berlioz through the Paganini
incident; how his courage was strengthened, and from a
morose, he became a cheerful companion. Then he
divulges what had been a life-secret: " Armand Bertin,
the wealthy and distinguished proprietor of the *Journal
des Débats*, had a high regard for Berlioz and knew of all
his struggles, which he, Bertin, was anxious to lighten.
He resolved therefore to make him a present of 20,000 fr.,
and in order to enhance the moral effect of this gift he
persuaded Paganini to appear as the donor of the money.
How well Bertin had judged was proved immediately;
what would have been a simple *gracieuseté* from a rich
and powerful editor towards one of his staff became a
significant tribute from one genius to another, and had a
colossal *retentissement*. The secret was well kept and
never divulged to Berlioz. It was known, I believe, to
but two of Bertin's friends besides myself, one of whom
is (Victor) Mottez, the celebrated painter; I learned it
about seven years later when I had become an intimate
friend of the house, and Madame Armand Bertin had
been for years one of my best pupils."* This must be
accepted as a true statement of the case, but it proves no
more than that Paganini became a party to a benevolent
conspiracy; he never boasted of the gift, nor claimed any
credit for it. Even when Berlioz, relieved of his financial

* Life and Letters of Sir Charles Hallé, p. 69.

troubles, set to work with a light heart at the composition which was to be worthy of dedication to the illustrious artist to whom he owed so much (his own words), even when he wrote to Paganini about a subject, all the answer he could get was : " I can give you no advice." He chose Shakespeare's " Romeo and Juliet " as a theme, worked at it for seven months, and produced a master-piece. Paganini inspired him, but never heard the work " undertaken chiefly to please him."

To Paganini the world owes still more. It has been already stated that Paganini's playing when in Paris in 1831 exerted an extraordinary influence over Franz Liszt, and gave the direction to his genius. I use the word " genius " advisedly, believing that Liszt is one of that sacred band to whom the term belongs of right. This is not the place to discuss the position Liszt occupies among composers ; nor is this country yet qualified properly to judge him. Wagner, Schumann and Chopin have passed the ordeal; from persecution they have arrived at deification, so to speak, and even their faults are regarded as merits. But prejudice dies hard, and Liszt has yet to suffer. His earnest disciple Walter Bache sacrificed time and means in his Liszt propaganda, but with scant success. My point here is to try and show that Paganini, despite all shortcomings as a man and as an artist, had a mission—whether he knew it or not—and fulfilled it through others.

Beethoven's pianoforte playing, and pianoforte com-positions, led makers of that instrument to extend its compass; Liszt led the way to a new system for the

pianoforte, with effects hitherto undreamt of, and the
impulse came from Paganini. No other instance is on
record of an instrument like the violin absolutely
revolutionising the treatment of the pianoforte. I have
already referred to Liszt in Paris, how, depressed and
suffering, he withdrew from art and buried himself in
solitude. The revolution of 1830 aroused him, but it was
Paganini who rekindled the flame of art. Here I must
have recourse to Lina Ramann's " Franz Liszt."

Liszt went to hear Paganini : " Charmed, stunned, yet
seeing clearly at the same time, he could have cried out
for sorrow and exultation. This playing ! it was the
vision of his soul, after which he had sought and grasped
and yet could never find or seize. Now here he felt it
realised before him. With kindling power it seized his
artistic will. Until then Liszt had groped and sought
without any conscious aim ; following the hidden impulse
of his spirit, he had given place to all kinds of whims. . . .
Now, all at once, he was led by Paganini into fixed paths
and the lost thread of his development was found again.
By Paganini's playing the veil had been torn away which
lay between him and his artistic will. . . . . Paganini's
playing had famed the Promethean spark of his genius to
a brilliant flame. That for which the poets of the time
strove in their literary productions—freedom of form and
of subject—he saw here in the domain of reproducing
music. With all this the serious defects and onesidedness
of the great violinist's capabilities and genius did not
escape the youthful pianist. He measured him by the
ideals of artistic culture which shone before his own

eyes. . . . . . He recognised plainly the limits of the influence which Paganini exercised over him, and saw how human was the mission of the artist—a consciousness was awakened that *artistic culture is inseparable from human sympathies, that only a great man can become a great artist.* This conviction drew from his lips the proud but noble words 'Génie oblige.'* With indescribable eagerness, and at the same time with exulting triumph, Liszt, after having heard Paganini, turned again to his instrument. He was seldom seen; in public, as a pianist, never. His mother alone was the silent witness of his perseverance and restless working. As Wieland, he hammered at his piano. He, who, already as a boy, had climbed the Parnassus of study, now sat at the instrument often six hours a day and practised; yes, he exercised the language of his spirit, and created for it an organ of expression." The author then goes on to describe the new ideas that came to Liszt when studying the Twenty-four Capricii of Paganini, and how he discovered new combinations, and also that the hand of the pianist had yet much to learn. " With this perception a bridge was built to new technical triumphs in the art of pianoforte playing. . . . . On the one hand he increased the beauty and breadth of sound of this instrument in a marvellous degree, while on the other, he gave at the same time a fatal blow to the modern pianoforte music of his day. This was the new discovery which Liszt made through Paganini, and on

---

* The last words of Liszt's article "Sur Paganini, A Propos de Sa Mort," published in the "Revue et Gazette Musicale de Paris," December 23, 1840.

the foundation of which he has created an extension of
the arena of sound. . . . . Thus Paganini's capriccios
gave Liszt the first impulse towards the modern system
for the pianoforte, and at the same time prompted him to
enter on the territory till then unknown of transferring
effects."*

What the influence of Liszt has been, is beyond the
present purpose to inquire. But, blot out Paganini and
every note he has written, and he reappears in the art
work of at least one great French composer, and in that
of the greatest pianist the world has yet seen—one to
whom the high compliment has been paid in the epithet
—"The Paganini of the Pianoforte."

---

* Franz Liszt, Artist and Man, Vol. I., pp. 258-65.

CHAPTER X.

IS it worth while at this distance of time to refer to the actual playing of Paganini? Can one recall "the touch of a vanished hand?" This memoir would not be complete without some account of Paganini's art beyond that given in the story of his life. Here I do not venture to write as a violin expert, and I shall only quote from Guhr's "On Paganini's Art of Playing the Violin" —which is presumably still accessible to students—in so far as it may be serviceable to the general reader. Leaving æsthetic, and higher considerations generally, out of count for the moment and limiting our attention to matters technical, we find much that was absolutely new. As regards mere extravagance and eccentricity of execution, Paganini was surpassed by Locatelli. We have to take into consideration the concert-pitch in use at the time of Paganini's public career. That, I take it, corresponded very closely with the Diapason normal now coming into general use. Paganini employed thin strings, and, for purposes to be named presently, often tuned his violin a semitone higher than the pitch of the band which accompanied him—equivalent to the English pitch, or high pitch still in use in some places. These thin strings

KING'S THEATRE

SIGNOR
PAGANINI'S
Sixth and Last,
GRAND CONCERT:
THIS EVENING
MONDAY, JUNE, 27th 1831.
PROGRAME

PART I

Overture in D . . . . *Rembers-*
Duetto signor Rubini, and Signor Santini, . . *Genesali.*
Grand Concerto in E flat. composed & performed by Signor Pagnini.
        1. Allegro Maestoso,
        2. Adagio Appassionato
        3. ronde Brilliante

Aria signor Petralia . . . . *Rossix.*
Overture Euranthe. . . . . *Weberi*

PART II

Sonata wth Variations on a Tema by Haydn. composed & performed
    ON ONE STRING
    the Fourth String by Signor PAGANINI,
Duetto, Signor Rubini and Signor santini, . . *Rossini.*
Cavantina, signor Petralia, Mercandante.
Prelude and Variations on the Tema. "Nel cor piu nonmissente"
    without orchestral accompaniment by
SIGNOR PAGANINI.
Overture Zaira, Winter.

    Conductor - - Signor M. Costa
    Leader. - - Signor Spagnoleti

The Prices of Boxes will be the same as on Opera Nights.
    ORCHESTRA AND STALLS,.....................£1 1s 6d.
    AD-ISSION to the PIT,............................0 10 6.
    ADMISSION to the GALLARY.....................0 0 0
  To commence at Half-past EIGHT o Clock, and the Doors to open One Hour before the Performance

    . Boxes, Stalls, and Tickets, may be had at the Box-Office, Haymarket

J. H. COX, Printer, 14, Garden Row, London Road, Southwark

PLATE 18. (*See Appendix.*)

THEATRE ROYAL
COVENT GARDEN.

The Nobility, Gentry, and the Public, are respectfully informed that arrangements
have been made with

SIGNOR
PAGANINI,

For a Series of Four Concerts;

THE FIRST OF WHICH WILL TAKE PLACE

THIS EVENING,

FRIDAY, JULY 6, 1832,

When he will perform three of his

FAVOURITE PIECES.

PART I.

GRAND OVERTURE to Die Zauberflöte. — — *Mozart.*
AIR, Mr. WILSON
CAVATINA, Signora PIETRALIA, 'Ah' s estmta " *(Donna Caradia)*
Mercadante

Grand Concerto,
ALLEGRO MAESTOSO,
Composed and performed by Signor PAGANINI.
AIR, Miss SHIRREFF, "The Soldier tired." *(Trumpet obligato, Mr. E. Harper.)*
Arne

PART II.

GRAND OVERTURE to *Der Freischütz.* — — *C. M. von Weber*
The celebrated Sonata (on the Prayer in Pietro L'Eremita,
followed by a Tema with Variations) composed and
performed on **ONE STRING ONLY,** (the Fourth String,) by
SIGNOR PAGANINI.
DUET, Mr. WILSON and Mr. MORLEY, " Love and War T. Cooke,
BALLAD Miss SHIRREFF. ' Faithful Ellen.' C. Horn
Variations on the Country Dance, **Delle Streghe alla noce di
Benevento,** (or the Comic Dance of the Witches under the
Walnut Tree of Benevento,) composed and performed by
SIGNOR PAGANINI,

Conductor, — SIR GEORGE SMART.
Leader of the Band, [with the kind permission of Capt. Polhill] **Mr. T. COOKE.**
Doors opened at HALF-PAST SEVEN O'CLOCK, the Concert to commence at EIGHT

Boxes 7s. Pit 3s. 6d. Galleries 2s

Applications for Boxes, Orchestra Seats, and Tickets to be made at the Box-Office, Hart-street

On Monday next,

Mademoiselle MARS,
Mademoiselle TAGLIONI,

will make their first appearance at this Theatre; when will be performed
VALERIE, ou LAVEUGLE.
The Principal Characters by Monsieur ARMAND, (from the Theatre Français, Paris,)
Mademoiselle St. ANGE, Monsieur LAPORTE, and
Mademoiselle MARS.
THE PETITE PIECE,
L'HERITAGE.
The Principal Characters by Monsieur ARMAND, and
Mademoiselle MARS.
And **TWO DIVERTISSEMENTS,**
In both which **Mademoiselle TAGLIONI** will appear
On Tuesday, SIGNOR PAGANINI'S SECOND CONCERT
Printed by W. REYNOLDS, 9, Exeter-street, Strand

PLATE 19. *(See Appendix.)*

Theatre Royal, Covent-Garden.

SIGNOR

PAGANINI's

FAREWELL

CONCERT

And positively the Last Night this Theatre will be open until the
commencement of the regular Dramatic Season,

THIS EVENING,

Friday, August 17, 1832,

When he will perform FOUR of his

FAVOURITE PIECES:

PART I.

GRAND SINFONIA. — — *Beethoven.*
ARIA, Signora PIETRALIA, "Elena, oh! tu ch'io chiamo." (*La Donna del Lago*)
[*Rossini.*
Grand Sonata Militare, in which will be introduced Mozart's
Aria, "Non piu andrai," followed by a Tema, with brilliant
Variations, (to conclude with "GOD SAVE THE KING!")
composed and to be performed on ONE STRING ONLY,
(the Fourth String,) by
SIGNOR PAGANINI.
ARIA, Mr. BENNETT, "Languir per una bella" *Rossini.*
AIR, Miss GEORGE, "Hours of sorrow." *Rossini.*
LARGHETTO e VARIAZIONE, on the favourite RONDO,
"Non piu mesta," in Rossini's Opera LA CENERENTOLA,
composed and to be performed by
SIGNOR PAGANINI.

PART II.

The CORONATION DUET, for the Harp and Piano-Forte.
Messrs. FREDERICK CHATTERTON and W. A. KING. *Bochsa.*
DUETTO; Signora PIETRALIA and Mr. BENNETT,
"Ah! se di mali miei." (*Il Tancredi*)—Rossini.
MAESTOSO SONATA SENTIMENTALE, with Variations
on Haydn's celebrated Tema "The Hymn to the Emperor,"
(to conclude with the National Air—"St. PATRICK's DAY,")
ON ONE STRING ONLY, (the Fourth String)
composed and to be performed by
SIGNOR PAGANINI.
RECIT. ed ARIA, Miss GEORGE, "Mi pizzica mi stimola."
(From *Auber's* Opera of *Masaniello*)—arranged by G. Penf.
BALLAD, Mr. BENNETT, "Fair is the morn." — *A. Lee.*
(BY DESIRE) Fandango Spagnuolo Variato, in which will be
introduced various Humorous Imitations of the Farm Yard,
Composed and to be performed by
Signor PAGANINI.

Leader of the Band, (with the kind consent of Capt. Polhill) Mr. T. COOKE.
Conductor, — SIR GEORGE SMART.

The Free List will be suspended, the Public Press excepted.

Doors opened at HALF-PAST SEVEN O'CLOCK, the Concert to commence at EIGHT.

Boxes 7s. Pit 3s. 6d. Galleries 2s

Printed by W. REYNOLDS, 9. Exeter-street, Strand.

PLATE 20. (*See Appendix.*)

☞ **THE LAST NIGHT**
of the Extraordinary Performance of

SIGNOR PAGANINI,

who has been again received with unbounded applause, by a full & fashionable audience.

THEATRE ROYAL, DRURY LANE.

The Nobility, Gentry, and the Public, are respectfully informed, that arrangements have been made with

SIGNOR
PAGANINI,

FOR A

Series of Four Concerts;

THE FOURTH AND LAST OF WHICH WILL TAKE PLACE

This Evening, WEDNESDAY, July 17, 1833,

In the course of which he will perform

Some of his most Established and Popular Pieces.

PART I.

GRAND OVERTURE TO WILLIAM TELL. .... (Rossini)
SONG. - Miss H. CAWSE. "*The Vesper Bell.*"
MARCH IN OTELLO, with Grand Variations and Orchestral Accompaniments, composed by HENRI HERZ, to be performed by Master MOUTRIE, aged Ten years, Pupil of HENRI HERZ.
Preludio e Rondo brilliante, composed and to be performed

By SIGNOR PAGANINI.

AIR. - Miss L A N D, "*Softly Nighs*" .... (WEBER.

PART II.

GRAND OVERTURE (M.S.) .... (Macfarren)
SONG. - Miss H. C A W S E, "*The Gay Troubador*"
RECITATIVO E TRE ARIE VARIATE, followed by the National Irish Air "St. Patrick's Day," on ONE STRING ONLY, (the Fourth String) composed and to be performed

By SIGNOR PAGANINI.

AIR. - Miss L A N D, '*Bid me Discourse*,
ARIA, Miss ELIZABETH JONAS, (eight years of age) "*Bravura Variatione,*" for the Grand Piano Forte (from the Opera of Joseph) (HERZ.)
By Desire, and in consequence of the enthusiastic applause bestowed on its performance last Evening, will be repeated,—
The humourous Variations on the Contra Danza "Delle Streghe," or the Comic Dance of the Witches, round the Walnut-tree of Benevento, composed and to be performed

By SIGNOR PAGANINI.

The Evening's Entertainments will conclude with the Ballet of The

Pages of The Duke de Vendome.

Duke de Vendôme, ... Mr. GILBERT,
Pages.—Victor, . . . -(Son of Marrmon) .... Miss BASÈKE,
Eugene. Miss HUNT, Philippe, Miss SHAW,

BOXES 7s. PIT 3s. 6d. GALLERY 2s.

• The Dramatic Free List of the Theatre does not extend to these Concerts, and every privilege (with the exception of the Public Press) must be suspended.*

The Doors will open at half-past Seven, and the Concert begin at Eight o'Clock.

On Friday,........ .... the Opera of **MASANIELLO.**
With the Third Act (in Italian) of Rossini's Opera of **OTELLO.**
To conclude with **THE MAID OF CASHMERE.** In which and during the Evening Madame Malibran Mesdemoiselles Fanny and Teresa Eisler, Madame Montessu Signor Donzelli, Monsieur Daumont, and Monsieur Albert will appear.
Being for the Benefit and Last Appearance in England of Mademoiselle AUGUSTA.

Pinsuti Rex et Regna S. G. Fairbrother, Printer, Theatre Royal Drury Lane

PLATE 21. (*See Appendix.*)

SIGNOR
PAGANINI

Respectfully informs the Nobility, Gentry, and Public of Shrewsbury and its Vicinity, that he will give a GRAND

CONCERT

AT THE LION BALL ROOM,

On Thursday, August 15th,

(Being positively the only Time he can possibly have the honour of performing before them previous to his Departure for the Court of St. Petersbourg), on which Occasion he has engaged those highly celebrated Vocalists—

MISS WELLS

AND

MISS WATSON,

LIKEWISE

MR. WATSON

(Composer to the Theatres Royal, English Opera House, and Covent Garden, and Member of the Royal Academy of Music).

PROGRAMME OF THE CONCERT.

ACT I.

Recit e Aria	Miss WELLS	" Il Braccio"	Niccolini.
Ballad	Miss WATSON	" Teach me to Forget"	Bishop.

Preludio e Rondo Brilliante } PAGANINI.
by Signor PAGANINI. }

Ballad	Miss WELLS	" John Anderson my Jo"	Melodies.
Song	Miss WATSON	" The Banks of Allan Water"	Mass

Grand Variations on the Air " Nel Cor Piu," } PAGANINI.
by Signor Paganini. }

ACT II.

Duett	Miss WELLS and Miss WATSON	" Sul 'Aria"	Mozart.

Sonata Militaire, entirely on one String } PAGANINI.
(the 4th), Signor Paganini. }

Ballad	Miss WELLS	" Away to the Mountain's Brow"	Lee
Ballad	Miss WATSON	" The Bonnee Wee Wife"	Miles
Melody of the North, by Miss WELLS and Miss WATSON		" The Keel Row"	Watson

The admired VARIAZIONI
upon the popular Neapolitan
Canzonetta, ' The Carnival of
Venice,' descriptive of the **PAGANINI.**
Freaks and Vagaries of a
Venetian Carnival, by Signor
PAGANINI.

Mr. WATSON will preside at the Piano Forte.

. Tickets, 7s. 6d. each, may be had of Mr. Eddowes, Bookseller, Corn Market.

The Concert will commence at Eight o'Clock precisely.

EDDOWES PRINTER, SHREWSBURY

PLATE 22. (*See Appendix.*)

served another purpose—the easy production of harmonics. If there was one thing more novel than any other in Paganini's playing it was the introduction of harmonics, melodies, double notes, and double shakes in harmonics. The natural harmonics were of course known to all violinists, but the artificial harmonics, if not the invention of Paganini, were first employed by him as integral features of his compositions as well as of his performances. Then there was his particular kind of *staccato,* produced by throwing his bow forcibly on the string, " letting it spring while he runs through the scales with incredible rapidity, the tones rolling like pearls " (Guhr). The Rev. Dr. Fox said the bow seemed to act with the elasticity of a spring fixed at one end, and made to vibrate. The combination of bowing, with *pizzicato* by the left hand, if not new, was employed by Paganini to a degree never attempted before. Lastly, there was his wonderful performance on the fourth string, which he tuned up to B flat, and sometimes even a semitone higher. Much of his use of these devices is put down as clap-trap, yet since his day many violinists have employed the same means, if they have not achieved the same result.

Let us consider, for a moment, the performances on the G string. It is certain that Paganini was not the originator of that manner of playing, for Leopold Mozart wrote of Esser* as playing on the G string alone with the greatest ease. Compositions for a single string were also written before Paganini's day, for Friedrich Wilhelm Rust (1739-1796) composed a violin sonata for the E

* Karl Michael Esser, born about 1736, date of death unknown.

string. But Paganini made such a feature of this species of performance because it pleased the public, and, in giving the audiences that which they preferred rather than that which his artistic conscience should have prompted, he became the pupil of his age, and fell from his high estate. On the other hand, he may be said to have discovered the powers of the fourth string, to which, by the employment of harmonics, he gave a compass of three octaves. He was censured for his partiality in this direction, but in these days every violinist plays a solo on the G string. Is not Bach's "Aria" played everywhere as a fourth string solo? Yet, as musicians know, it was not written for that string, nor as a solo, forming, as it does, the theme of the slow movement of the "Overture in D," for strings, two oboes, three trumpets, and drums. Moreover, in Mozart's Violin Concerto in E flat, No. 6, composed in 1766, there is in the slow movement, an eight-bar period for the G string, and also one of the same length in the Finale. In Beethoven's Violin Concerto the principal theme of the Rondo is assigned to the G string, and also when it recurs after the second subject. This work was composed in 1806, a short time after Paganini wrote his "Napoleon Sonata," but was heard in public years before Paganini's was so performed. These two compositions are mentioned merely to show that the charm of the fourth string was not unknown in early days; to refer to later works would be superfluous.

Now, as to Paganini's tuning his instrument a semitone higher than the ordinary pitch. It will be conceded that

the different keys have distinctive qualities, to which
some musicians are more sensitive than others. Some
term it key-colour : I prefer the expression key-character.
On the violin some keys are more sonorous than others.
The effect may be partly mental, and I believe—though
I may be wrong—that a violinist plays with a different
feeling in the key of E, to that which would be excited
by the key of E flat, and this apart from the æsthetic
import of the composition itself.* In many concertos the
chorus violins—if I may so call them—sometimes play
the same notes with the soloist, and so absorb the tone of
the latter that the listener can only hear the mass of
violin tone. It is on record that Paganini was never
overpowered by the *tutti* in any of the pieces he played,
though some writers say his tone was not remarkable for
volume. The explanation may be found in what follows.
Paganini had an almost morbidly keen musical organisa-
tion, an acute sense of hearing, in which he resembled
Mozart and Berlioz. Paganini wrote the solo part of his
first concerto in D (tuning his violin a semitone higher),
and the orchestral parts in E flat. Why ? Not because
D was an easier key to play in, nor because some
passages if viewed as in E flat were marvels of execution ; but because he felt the difference in the "power"
of the two keys. Mozart's Concertante for violin and
viola, with orchestra, is in E flat, but the viola part is in
D, and the instrument was to be tuned a semitone higher.
This was done "both to give it a clear sound and to make

---

* In the Tonic Sol-fa method great stress is laid upon the mental
effect of each note of the scale, altogether apart from pitch.

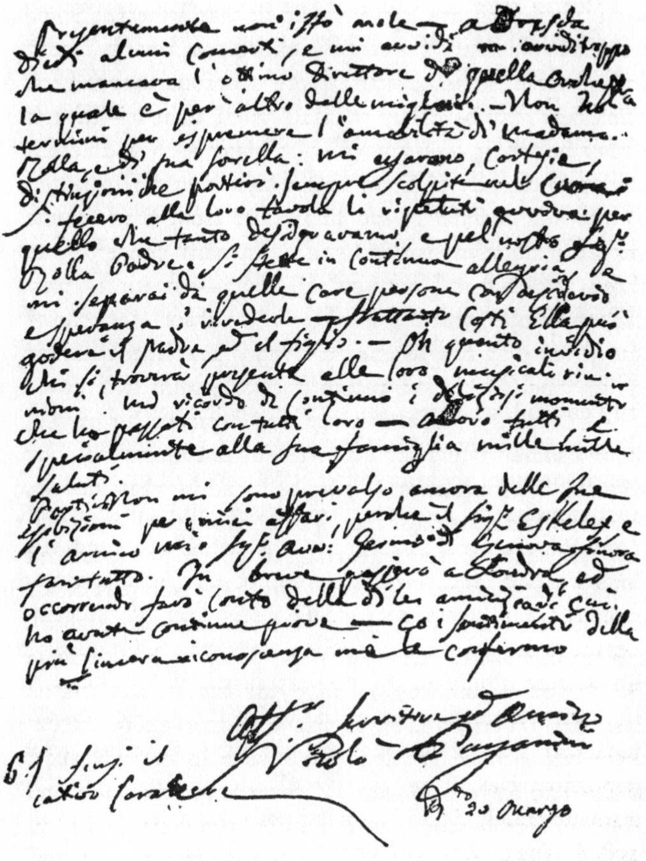
[illegible]entemente [illegible] molto a Dresda
diedi alcuni Concerti, e mi accorsi [illegible] troppo
che mancava l'ottimo Direttore di quella Orchestra
la quale è per altro delle migliori. — Non ho
termini per esprimere l'amabilità di Madama
[illegible], e di sua sorella: mi usarono cortesie,
distinzioni che porterò sempre scolpite nel cuore:
si [illegible] alla loro tavola li rispettati [illegible] per
quello che tanto desideravano, e pel nostro Sig.r
[illegible] Padre. Si stette in continua allegria, e
mi separai da quelle care persone con desiderio
e speranza di rivederle [illegible] Ella può
godere il padre ed il figlio. — Oh quanto invidio
chi si troverà presente alle loro musicali [illegible]
[illegible] ricordo di continuo i deliziosi momenti
che ho passati con tutti loro — A loro tutti e
specialmente alla sua famiglia mille e mille
saluti.
[illegible] Non mi sono prevalso ancora delle sue
esibizioni per i miei affari, perchè il Sig.r Eskeles e
l'amico mio Sig.r Avv: Germi di Genova sinora
fan tutto. In breve passerò a Londra, ed
occorrendo farò conto della di lei amicizia di cui
ho avute continue prove — Coi sentimenti della
più sincera riconoscenza mi le confermo

Aff.mo Servitore ed Amico
[illegible] Paganini

[illegible] 20 Marzo

[illegible]

PLATE 23. (*See Appendix.*)

the execution easier."* Mozart's piece was probably
written in 1780, so here is one of the expedients ascribed
to Paganini as a trick made use of by a great master
before the famous violinist was born. Berlioz never
heard Paganini play, but he was the first among his
contemporaries to understand and appreciate Paganini's
intention in this respect. In his *Soirées de l'Orchestre* he
wrote : " He (Paganini) has known how to render distinct
and dominating the tones of a solo violin by tuning its
four strings a semitone above those of the orchestra ;
which enabled him to play in the brilliant keys of D and
A, while the orchestra accompanied him in the less
sonorous keys of E flat and B flat." Berlioz knew, if
any one did, what was the distinctive character of a key.
It is highly improbable that either he or Paganini ever
heard, or even knew anything of Mozart's "Concertante"
just mentioned. So much by way of clearing Paganini
from the charge of charlatanry. Artistic faults and fail-
ings he had, and these no attempt has been made to
conceal; but every succeeding generation of violinists
has been deeply indebted to the great Genoese for opening
up new possibilities, by the way in which he advanced
the character and power of the violin. Leaving now the
technical side of his art, let us hear what his great
contemporaries have to say of his playing from the
æsthetic standpoint. We need not refer again to Lafont
and Lipinski, but will begin with Spohr. It has been
mentioned that Spohr met Paganini at Venice, in 1816.
Spohr wished to hear the great Italian play something,

* Life of Mozart, Otto Jhan, English Edition, I., 319.

but the latter declined. He afterwards explained to Spohr that his style of playing was calculated for the great public only; and that if he were to play to Spohr he must play in a different manner, for which he was not then inclined. So it was not until 1830 that Spohr heard Paganini at Cassel. This is what he wrote: " In June, 1830, Paganini came to Cassel and gave two concerts in the theatre, which I heard with great interest. His left hand, and his constantly pure intonation were to me astonishing. But in his compositions and his execution, I found a strange mixture of the highly genial and childishly tasteless, by which one felt alternately charmed and disappointed, so that the impression left as a whole was, after frequent hearing, by no means satisfactory to me." Paganini was playing to his "great public," and in that respect lost Spohr's esteem; but can a great violinist, of strong personality, be perfectly just to a contemporary of a different temperament? Schumann, as a composer, could look upon Paganini from a different point of view. This is what he says: "When I heard him for the first time, I expected him to begin with a tone such as had never been heard before. But with how small, how thin a tone he commenced! Then he began to weave his spells; invisibly he threw out his magnetic chains among the public; they oscillated above and around. And then the rings became more and more intricate; even the audience seemed to contract, while he interlaced his tones until they seemed melted into one—one with the master himself, all counterbalancing each other with sympathetic influence." This is not criticism; it is scarcely descrip-

tion: it is as fanciful as Heinrich Heine's description,
but it is a proof of the great violinist's power to touch the
imagination. Ignaz Moscheles, a virtuoso pianist, com-
plains of his utter inability to find language capable of
conveying a description of Paganini's wonderful performance. " Had that long-drawn, soul-searching tone lost
for a single second its balance, it would have lapsed into
a discordant cat's-mew; but it never did so, and
Paganini's tone was always his own, and unique of its
kind. The thin strings of his instrument—on which
alone it was possible to conjure forth those myriads of
notes and thrills and cadenzas—would have been fatal in
the hands of any other violin player, but with him they
were indispensable adjuncts." Again: "Nothing could
exceed my surprise and admiration; his constant and
venturesome flights, his newly discovered source of
flageolet tones, his gift of fusing and beautifying subjects
of the most heterogeneous kind; all these phases of
genius so completely bewildered my musical perceptions,
that for several days afterwards my head seemed on fire
and my brain reeled. I never wearied of the intense
expression, soft and melting like that of an Italian singer,
which he could draw from his violin." Yet, later,
Moscheles had to say: " I find both his style and manner
of playing monotonous." Liszt, many years later said:
" No one who has not heard him can form the least idea
of his playing." Paganini indeed could soar to the
Empyrean, but he had not the Peri's pure gift which
would open the gate of Paradise !

François Joseph Fétis, who befriended Paganini when

first he visited Paris, certainly held no brief for the celebrated artist, but rather presided over him as judge. He stated that the art of Paganini was an art apart, which was born with him, and of which he carried the secret to the grave. He futher stated that Paganini often assured him that his talent was the result of a secret discovered by himself, a secret he intended to reveal, before his death, in a method for the violin, which should have but few pages, but which should throw all violinists into confusion. Fétis questions the existence of the secret, and thinks the great artist was labouring under a delusion. Yet he has to acknowledge that there was something extraordinary and mysterious in the power that Paganini possessed in the execution of unheard of difficulties in an infallible manner. His intonation was always perfect.*

William Gardiner, the Leicester amateur, who became acquainted with Paganini, wrote: "There was no trick in his playing; it was all fair, scientific execution, opening to us a new order of sounds, the highest of which ascended two octaves above C in alt."

An Italian physician, Francesco Bennati,† made a physiological study of Paganini, accounting for his wonderful executive powers as due not so much to his

---

* In 1883, several musical papers stated that a certain amateur collector of violins, during a tour in Italy, visited the little Sardinian village, Ameglia, and purchased a collection of instruments used by Paganini, which were at that time in the possession of the widow of L. M. Germi, the intimate friend of Paganini. The said amateur also became possessed of " the secret," but what he did with it has never transpired.

† Born at Mantua, 1798; died at Paris, 1834.

musical genius as to his peculiar physical formation. In particular, the flexibility of his wrist, and the great lateral extension of his finger joints, enabled him to execute passages impossible to others. But there must have been something beyond technique. I have heard many persons, professional and amateur, speak of his playing as something beyond conception, not only in regard to execution, but in the power of swaying an audience, playing upon their emotions; the whole man was an instrument. No other artist was so widely quoted by his contemporaries. Mendelssohn, Chopin, and others make reference to Paganini whenever anything wonderful is spoken of. Chopin was a great admirer of Slavik, and considered him only second to Paganini. Every volume of reminiscences down to the present day includes the name of Paganini, if only to relate that somebody once heard him play. But not only musicians, poets also sang his praises. Is there anything more beautiful than the tribute paid him by Leigh Hunt? A few lines may be quoted :

> So played of late to every passing thought
> With finest change (might I but half as well
> So write !) the pale magician of the bow,
> Who brought from Italy the tales made true,
> Of Grecian lyres, and on his sphery hand,
> Loading the air with dumb expectancy,
> Suspended, ere it fell, a nation's breath.
>
> He smote—and clinging to the serious chords
> With godlike ravishment, drew forth a breath,
> So deep, so strong, so fervid thick with love,
> Blissful, yet laden as with twenty prayers,
> That Juno yearn'd with no diviner soul
> To the first burthen of the lips of Jove.

The exceeding mystery of the loveliness
Sadden'd delight ; and with his mournful look,
Dreary and gaunt, hanging his pallid face
'Twixt his dark and flowing locks, he almost seem'd,
To feeble or to melancholy eyes,
One that had parted with his soul for pride,
And in the sable secret liv'd forlorn.

But true and earnest, all too happily
That skill dwelt in him, serious with its joy ;
For noble now he smote the exulting strings,
And bade them march before his stately will ;
And now he lov'd them like a cheek, and laid
Endearment on them, and took pity sweet ;
And now he was all mirth, or all for sense
And reason, carving out his thoughts like prose
After his poetry ; or else he laid
His own soul prostrate at the feet of love,
And with a full and trembling fervour deep,
In kneeling and close-creeping urgency,
Implored some mistress with hot tears ; which past,
And after patience had brought right of peace,
He drew as if from thoughts finer than hope
Comfort around him in ear-soothing strains
And elegant composure ; or he turn'd
To heaven instead of earth, and raise a prayer
So earnest-vehement, yet so lowly sad,
Mighty with want and all poor human tears,
That never saint, wrestling with earthly love,
And in mid-age unable to get free,
Tore down from heaven such pity.

It was urged against Paganini as a fault, that he rarely played any other music than his own. Paganini was one of the latter-day examples of the virtuoso and the composer represented by one and the same person. From the days of Handel to the time of Beethoven, the composer was his own interpreter, and never gave concerts with compositions by others. But Paganini did

at times play concertos by Rode and Kreutzer, though it
was said that in these he was less successful than in his
own. The Rev. Dr. Cox heard Paganini play the first
movement of Beethoven's Concerto—in fact it was performed for his special edification. This is what he said
of it: "Never shall I forget the smile on that sad, pale,
wan, and haggard face, upon every lineament of which
intense pain was written in the deepest lines, when I
caught his eye, or the playing, into which a spirit and
sympathy were thrown that carried one wholly away. As
soon as he had concluded, and before I could rush up to
him to express my thanks, he glided away. I never saw
him afterwards." It was also stated that Paganini failed
as a quartet player. His strong individuality might have
been an obstacle in the way of securing the perfect
unanimity of feeling and expression that characterise fine
quartet playing; but to imply that he could not perform
the music was absurd. As an executant, pure and simple,
Paganini never had, and possibly never may have, a
compeer.

But the question remains: did Paganini's playing
result in any permanent benefit to the art? Had he a
permanent influence, and if so, was it for good? To take
a material aspect, it was owing to Paganini that the fame
of Joseph Guarnerius was published beyond Italy. "The
names of Amati and Stradivarius became familiar to the
musical world gradually, but Guarnerius, in the hands of
a Paganini, came forth at a bound. This illustrious
violin was often credited with the charm which belonged
to the performer; the magical effects and sublime strains

Plate XXIV.—See Appendix.

A Semi-Caricature of Paganini, 1831.

that he drew forth from it, must, it was thought, rest in the violin. Every would-be violinist, whose means permitted him to indulge in the luxury, endeavoured to secure an instrument by the great Guarnerius. The demand thus raised brought forth those gems of the violin maker's art now in the possession of wealthy amateurs and a few professors. When the various works of the gifted Guarnerius were brought to light, much surprise was felt that such treasures should have been known only to a handful of obscure players, chiefly in the churches of Italy."*

It has been shown that Paganini's performances caused a revolution in the style of composition and execution in pianoforte music, as exemplified in the works of Liszt. But did violin playing benefit? As Paganini belonged to no school, so he founded no school. He had his imitators, but he had few pupils, and no absolute successor. Camillo Sivori is generally put forth as his only pupil. I have heard that great artist, but—I say it with diffidence—I could never consider him the equal of what I imagined Paganini to have been. According to William Gardiner, Paganini was accompanied by Antonio Oury when he first went to London. It was Oury who introduced Gardiner to Paganini, and the former stated that Oury was Paganini's favourite pupil.† Then the Chevalier

---

* "The Violin," by George Hart. Popular Edition, 1880, p. 202.

† It is strange that the Biographical Dictionaries are silent concerning Oury, who must have been a man of some note. He is merely named as the husband of Anna Caroline de Belleville, the once famous pianist (1806-1880), who made her début in London at a Paganini concert in 1831.

Robbio, who appeared at Jullien's concerts at Drury
Lane Theatre in 1854, claimed to have been a pupil of
Paganini. Acknowledged pupils were Teresa Ottavio,
who was playing in Vienna, in 1835, and Mlle. Neumann,
who gave concerts in Venice and elsewhere, in 1838.
But all these were of small account. The question
remains. Did Paganini influence the art of violin playing,
and in what direction? Let a very recent writer con-
tribute an answer. "We would not miss this greatest of
fiddlers in the annals of violin playing—no, not for a
Spohr or any other great modern violin master; but his
influence can hardly be called beneficial. It forced
violin playing into a Procrustean bed unsuited to its true
nature and mission. Paganini had temporarily transformed the angel into a devil, and the angel did not
escape unscathed—Lucifer burned his wings. Violin-
playing will never be quite what it was before Paganini.
He helped to hurry the growing old process—brought
out the lines, the spots, and the wrinkles on the once fair
face. He, before all others, established the iron rule of
technique, with its train of other evils, in the place of the
gentler reign of charming naiveté of the elder master."*
There is truth here, and cause for sadness; but can the
hand of time be turned back, and music regain the artless
joy of the seventeenth century, when technique was
unknown? Paganini, after all, was only one of the
forces that effected the revolution that produced the
music of the last half of the nineteenth century. It is
not too much to say that the technique of the modern

---

* The Story of the Violin by Paul Stoeving, p. 208.

orchestra, in regard to the string section, is due to Paganini. Compare the scores of the classical composers with those of the most modern writers, and see what an enormous difference there is in the work for the strings—from the violins to the double-basses. The orchestral player of to-day is a virtuoso. For good or evil, music has entered upon a phase that has raised executive skill to a pinnacle never attained before: and this it owes to Paganini: may it be the prelude to higher achievements in the spiritual domain of art!

CHAPTER XI.

THERE remains the consideration of Paganini as a composer. It is a truism to say that a composition has primarily to be judged from the standpoint of the age in which it was written. A Genius, we are told, is not only before his own age, but before all ages. All the same, the great Geniuses come into the world precisely at the right moment. To some music one may fitly apply the epithet "Immortal"; for it seems to be written, "not for an age, but for all time." That title is not claimed for the music of Paganini, but, in view of what has been written for the violin, it is necessary to take into consideration the date of Paganini's compositions. Take the two greatest surviving forms—the symphony and the concerto—and compare works in those forms, belonging to different periods. Mendelssohn and Schumann were innovators, so it was said, in regard to symphonic form. Both wrote symphonies of which the movements were connected, and Schumann by the recurrence of themes anticipated the "organic whole" of the symphonic poem. But in 1776, Carl Philipp Emanuel Bach composed symphonies in the modern one-movement style. This is not the time to discuss them, but just

taking the first, in D, I may point to the coda of the
opening movement, which effects a modulation to E flat,
the key of the slow movement. In this the subject
enters, for the second time, in B flat; and a deceptive
cadence is followed by a passage ending on the dominant
of D, and so returning to the primary key for the last
movement. The score is for flutes, oboes, one bassoon,
horns, first and second violins, viola, violoncello, violone,
and cembalo. Now, here is a work quite modern in its
disregard of key relationship, and in the linking together
of the different movements. Yet it would not be right to
judge it by comparison with the symphonies of the last
half century.

With regard to the concerto, take that form for the
violin only. To go no further back than the works of the
great Leipzig Cantor, Johann Sebastian Bach, we find
his two concertos, in A minor, and E major, are scored
only for strings, though the " continuo " implies the
harpsichord. The concerto in D minor for two violins is
scored in the same manner; and in all there is evidence
that the soloist took part in the *tutti* sections. Then
there is the Symphony movement, from an unknown
church cantata, for violin concertante, with accompaniment
of two oboes, three trumpets, drums, two violins, viola
and continuo. In all these the basic principle is the
contrasting of the *tutti* and *solo* sections, which sustain a
kind of dialogue. Much the same form is observed in
Mozart's violin concertos, which, with one exception, are
scored for oboes, horns and strings. The exception is the
sixth, in E flat, which is scored for one flute, two oboes,

bassoons, and horns. In this the form approaches that of the sonata, though the *tutti* and *solo* contrasts still remain, and evidently the soloist played in the *tutti* sections. To Viotti, born in 1753, three years before Mozart, must be assigned the honour of giving the violin concerto its fullest classical form. His orchestral background was rich in colour, he having adopted the complete Haydn Combination; and his solo parts were of prime importance. Beethoven's concerto (1806), and Mendelssohn's (finished in 1844), employ the same orchestra. Beethoven links the slow movement to the Finale, and Mendelssohn connects the whole. The latest concerto form is in part a reversion to the earliest type. The solo part is but a more elaborate line in the orchestral column, and the soloist is scarcely distinguishable from his orchestral colleagues.

In view of the question I wish to raise, I hope the reader will pardon this digression. Paganini sometimes played pieces by Kreutzer and Rode, but I have not been able to find evidence of his acquaintance with the concertos of Viotti. The reason may not be far to seek. Paganini remained in Italy until 1828; Viotti, born in Italy, left his country, and only once returned to it—in 1783, and that for a very short time. His long residence in Paris led to his being identified with the French School of violinists. His works were played by other performers during his life-time, but it is questionable whether they were known to Paganini. What I want to ask is simply this:—upon what work, or whose work, was Paganini's first concerto modelled? It was written in 1811, according to the *Musical World* (Vol. for 1851, p. 822), or in 1820 according to the "Oxford History of Music" (Vol. VI., p. 225). The form of the work will be dealt with later; here the question is one of instrumentation. Berlioz wrote: "It was said of Weber, 'He is a meteor!' With equal justice it may be said of Paganini, 'He is a comet!'" I would paraphrase Berlioz and say Paganini's First Concerto came upon the world as a comet—a comet with a most portentous tail! Paganini was the Richard Strauss of his day. Fancy, in the scoring of a concerto, trombones, double-bassoon, cymbals, and bass-drum! and that in the year 1811, possibly. Why, it only requires a few more horns and trumpets, some tubas, a rattle and other percussion instruments, to come up to the latest twentieth century scoring. But a truce to badinage. A big score, of itself, is not necessarily a thing to be praised; however, Paganini's full scoring never obscured the solo part, and that is more than can be said of some violin concertos of later date. I do not pretend to a knowledge of the whole of the literature for the violin, but I have heard much of it; yet I can recall no violin concerto going beyond the orchestral resources adopted by Beethoven in his work, of earlier date than Paganini's first concerto. I have further to confess that I have never seen an original score of any of Paganini's works, but I have written out a score from what I believe to be authentic band parts. I have heard the First Concerto, "reduced to one act," with the exordium cut out; and however much such a rendering may be in accordance with modern taste, I can only regard it as unjust to the

composer. In the present day Paganini's music is looked
upon with pity not far removed from scorn; how did his
contemporaries esteem it ?

Rossini is reported to have said : " Truly, it is fortunate
that Paganini did not devote himself exclusively to lyric
composition ; he would have become a very dangerous
rival."* Moscheles wrote : " His concertos are beautiful,
and have even their grand moments; but they remind
me of a brilliant firework on a summer's eve, one flash
succeeding the other—effective, admirable—but always
the same. His 'Sonate Militaire,' and other pieces, have
a southern glow about them, but this hero of the violin
cannot dispense with the roll of the drum ; and completely
as he may annihilate his less showy colleagues, I long for
a little of Spohr's earnestness, Baillot's power, and even
Mayseder's piquancy."

Very little was said of Paganini's compositions—I
mean by way of description, orchestration, or even
criticism—when the composer was in England. The
writers seemed always engrossed and absorbed by the
performance and personality of the man.

Schumann repeats what was said of Paganini; that he,
himself, rated his merit as a composer more highly than
his talent as a *virtuoso*. We know that Rubinstein desired
to have his name handed down to posterity as a composer
rather than as a pianist. The fates have been unkind to
both. To return to Schumann. He remarks that " if
general opinion has not, until now, agreed with him
(Paganini), it must at least be allowed that his composi-

* Lapheléque, p. 45.

tions contain many pure and precious qualities, worthy of
being firmly fixed in the richer setting required by the
pianoforte." This of course referred to the caprices,
Op. 1, but the observation is a curious illustration of the
way in which individual minds regard things from their
own standpoint.

Paganini's music appealed to Liszt as a means of
creating a new school of pianoforte technique, as well as
composition; very little can be gleaned from Liszt as to
his æsthetic views regarding it.   Fétis says great worth
is revealed in the compositions of Paganini, as much by
the novelty of the ideas as by the elegance of the form,
the richness of the harmony, and the effects of the
instrumentation.   These qualities shine above all in the
concertos; but, he adds, these works require the magic
of his talent to produce the effect he intended.   Berlioz
was, perhaps, the most appreciative of Paganini's con
temporaries.   In his *Soirées de l'Orchestre* he says: "A
volume might be written in telling all that Paganini has
created in his works of novel effect, ingenious con-
trivances, noble and grandiose forms, and orchestral
combinations unknown before his time.   His melodies
are broad Italian melodies, but full of a passionate ardour
seldom found in the best pages of dramatic composers of
his country.   His harmonics are always clear, simple,
and of extraordinary sonorousness.   His orchestration is
brilliant and energetic, without being noisy.   He often
introduces the bass drum into his *tutti* with unusual
intelligence."

During Paganini's lifetime no one else seems to have

played his music, although one of his imitators is said to
have reproduced some pieces from memory.   After
Paganini's death, the propagandist of his works was his
nephew and pupil, Ernesto Camillo Sivori.   He made his
début at the Leipzig Gewandhaus Concerts, October 3,
1841, and a week later introduced there Paganini's
Variations on the Prayer from *Mosé in Egitto*.   In all,
some dozen pieces by Paganini were given at those
famous concerts from 1841 to 1876.   Sivori also introduced Paganini to the then very conservative concerts of
the Philharmonic Society, London, in 1844.   But they
did strange things in those days.   The first movement of
the Concerto in B minor was included in the first part of
the concert on April 29, 1844; the Adagio and Rondo
coming in the middle of the second part!   Poor Sivori
had to submit to similar treatment of his own concerto at the Society's concerts in 1845.   It would be
interesting to know how Paganini's music fared at the
concerts of the Paris Conservatoire, but I have not
been able to procure any reliable data relating to the
subject.

Rumour was long busy with the project entertained by
Paganini's son, the Baron Achilles, of publishing a
complete edition of the compositions of the great
violinist; and in 1887 a paragraph in the *Athenæum*
announced on apparently good authority that the Baron
was preparing for immediate publication the whole of the
works of his father which still remained in manuscript.
Several of those were named, but nothing more has been
heard of the undertaking.   I have scrutinised the musical

press from that date to the present time, and have failed to gather any further information on the subject.

From every available source I have compiled the following list of Paganini's compositions :—

Op. 1. Twenty-four Capriccios, for violin alone.
Op. 2. Six Sonatas, for violin and guitar.
Op. 3. Six Sonatas, for violin and guitar.
Op. 4. Three Grand Quartets, for violin, viola, violoncello and guitar.
Op. 5. Three Grand Quartets, for the same.
Op. 6. Concerto, No. 1, in E flat (D), for violin and orchestra.
Op. 7. Concerto, No. 2, in B minor, for the same.
Op. 8. "Le Streghe." Introduction and Variations.
Op. 9. "God Save the King." Variations.
Op. 10. "Carnaval de Venise." Variations.
Op. 11. "Allegro de Concert." "Moto Perpetuo."
Op. 12. "Non più mesta." Introduction and Variations.
Op. 13. "Di tanti palpiti." Introduction and Variations.
All for violin and orchestra.
Op. 14. Sixty Studies in Variation form, on the Air "Barucaba," for violin alone.

Works without Opus number.

Sonata in A, for violin, with accompaniment of violin and violoncello.
Bravura Variations on a theme from Rossini's "Moses in Egypt," for violin and string quartet, or pianoforte.
Bravura Variations on an Original Theme, for violin and guitar, or pianoforte.
Introduction and Variations on the Theme, "Nel cor più non mi sento," for violin alone.
Duo in C major, for one violin. Solo.
Recitative and Variations, on Three Airs, for the fourth string.
"Le Charme de Padua," Divertissement, for violin and pianoforte.

Works that are unpublished, or that have been lost.

Concertos in D minor, E minor, E major.
Concerto in two movements. Violin and orchestra.
Four Concertos, the scoring unfinished.

Concerto, for bassoon, with string trio accompaniment.
Nine Quartets, for violin, viola, violoncello and guitar.
Fantasia. Violin and orchestra.
Dramatic Sonata, " The Storm," for the same.
Military Sonata on Mozart's " Non più andrai."
Napoleon Sonata for the fourth string.
Sonata on a Theme by Haydn. Ditto.
Sonata di un Canto Appassionata, e variazioni sopra un Tema
    Marziale. Ditto.
Sonata with variations on a Theme from Jos. Weigl's " L'Amor
    Marinaro."
Sonata Amorosa Galante, e Tema con variazioni.
Sonata for viola and orchestra.
Sonata Sentimentale.
Sonata, " Varsovie."
Sonata for violin alone.
Preludio e Rondo brilliant, violin and orchestra.
Chant of the Monks of the Monastery of St. Bernard.
" La Primavera," Sonata for violin alone.
Preludio e Fandango, con Variazioni.
" La ci darem la Mano," Variations.
Cantabile, violin and pianoforte.
Polonaise avec variations.
Cantabile e Valse.
Cantabile, for two strings.
Three duos, violin and violoncello.
Duets and small pieces for guitar.
Variations sur un thème comique.
" The Vagaries of a Farm Yard."

Romance pour le Chant.
Fantasie Vocale.

WORKS WITH OPUS NUMBER.

Op. 1. The full title reads:—*Ventiquattro Caprici per
Violino solo, dedicati agli artisti ; Opera prima.* It is not
necessary to refer to these pieces in detail; they are in
the repertory of the leading violinists, and have been
played by Joachim and many others. They embrace

almost every kind of violin technique, and have merits apart from that standpoint. Schumann in his *Etudés d'apres les Caprices de Paganini*, Op. 3, has transcribed for the pianoforte six numbers. They are, No. 5, Agitato, in A minor, without the alteration of a single note; No. 9, Allegretto in E, quite as closely; the Andante of No. 11, in C; No. 13, Allegro, in B flat, beautifully harmonized; No. 19, Lento, Allegro assai, in E flat, more freely treated; and No. 16, Presto, in G minor, the melody assigned to the left hand, and written two octaves lower. These studies were the result of Schumann's hearing Paganini at Frankfort in 1830. The impression the great violinist made on the susceptible youth was so deep, that Wasielewski stated that it was more than probable Schumann's decision to devote himself to music dated from that experience. So here is another debt the musical world owes to Paganini. Schumann's Op. 3 bears the date of 1832. The next year he returned to the Italian master, and his Six Studies, Op. 10, are further transcriptions of the Capriccios. The first is a very free arrangement of No. 12, Allegro molto, in A flat; next is a paraphrase of No. 6, Adagio, in G minor, in which different figuration was absolutely necessary for the keyboard instrument. In No. 10, Vivace, in G minor, he divides the melody for the two hands, and accompanies with bold harmonies. The transcription of No. 4, Maestoso, in C, is almost literal, but there are "cuts," as also in No. 12. No. 2, Moderato, in B minor, with its "leaps and bounds," is altered to bring the intervals more within reach of the hand. The bare octaves which form

the opening of No. 3, have been filled in with rich
harmonies, and to the Presto movement a counterpoint in
semiquavers has been added, making it a very attractive
piece of the Tocatta order. It will be remembered that
one short movement of Schumann's "Carnival" is
entitled Paganini, but it is a reflexion of his style rather
than an adaptation of his music. Liszt has borrowed
much, in regard to form and melodic outline, from the
Capriccios, in his *Etudés d'exécution transcendante*. Of his
Grandes Etudes de Paganini notice will be taken later.
Brahms has written two sets of variations on the theme
of the Capriccio, No. 24, Quasi presto, in A minor.
These are extraordinarily difficult and brilliant. They
were published in 1866, and Carl Tausig was fond of
playing them. Paganini's Op. 1, was published by
Ricordi about the year 1820.

Op. 2, and Op. 3. The house of Ricordi publish the
Twelve Sonatas for violin and guitar, and Breitkopf and
Härtel publish an edition for violin and pianoforte, edited
by Ferdinand David. There is no clue as to the arranger
of the pianoforte part, but it may be the work of
Moscheles, who, it will be remembered, was induced "to
make a pianoforte accompaniment for twelve small violin
pieces," but who refused to have his name affixed to the
title-page. Anyway, the pianoforte accompaniment is
the work of a good musician. The title page of Op. 2
runs thus : *Sei Sonate per Violino e chitarra, Composte e
Dedicate Al Signor Dellepiane, Da Nicolo Paganini*. The
pieces are sonatas in the primitive sense of the term.
Each contains two movement only. No. 1, Minuetto,

Adagio in A, three-four, the violin part in the nature of a florid *cadenza* but very clear in rhythm, the guitar accompaniment in semiquaver groups of broken chords. Second movement, Polonese, Quasi allegro, A major, three-four, tuneful, all derived from a short motive, not difficult. No. 2, Larghetto expressivo, C major, six-eight, lyrical, melody highly embellished after the first phrase, varied bowing. Allegro spiritoso, same key and measure, in the style of a *Canto popolare*. No. 3, Adagio maestoso, D minor, two-four, principal motive of a dramatic kind, with brilliant passages intervening. Andantino gallantement, a crisp, staccato melody, with middle section in D major. No. 4, Andante calcando, A major, four-two, theme, in sixths, thirds and octaves. The movement is entitled *La Sinagoga*, but I can trace no Jewish melody corresponding to its subject. The second movement, Andantino con brio, in two-four measure is as bright and sparkling as the corresponding movement in No. 3. No. 5, Andante moderato, D major, two-four, two strains of eight bars, with a lyrical theme. The second movement in six-eight rhythm, is another specimen of the Italian *Cantilena*. No. 6, Largo, A minor, six-eight, a combination of recitative and Cadenza passages. Tempo di Valse, in three-eight measure, a tripping, fluent theme, for light bowing. The music altogether is light and pleasing, abounding in showy passages, and with the real Italian gift of melody. The accompaniments are in no way difficult.

The Six Sonatas, Op. 3, have rather a curious dedication: *Alla Ragazza Eleonora*. " Ragazza " is a familiar

term for a girl, and may be translated as "lass," or even
"wench." The Eleonora it may be impossible now to
identify, though the lady possibly was connected with
the period of Paganini's disappearance when Napoleon
invaded Italy. Sonata, No. 1, is in two movements, as
are all the others. The first, Larghetto, A major, six-
eight measure, has a theme resembling a popular melody,
the close of each strain being highly embellished.
Ricordi's edition gives an alternative reading of the
penultimate bar, in the style of a cadenza. The second
movement, Presto variato, in two-four rhythm, has a
dance-like theme, with one variation. The two bars
preceding the final cadence have semiquaver groups to
be played pizzicato, each note with right and left hand
alternately. No. 2, Adagio, con dolcezza, G major,
three-eight, theme, pure Italian cantilena, in thirds or
sixths throughout. Andantino scherzoso, two-four, crisp,
tripping melody, chiefly for staccato bowing, ending with
arpeggios extending to four octaves. No. 3, Andante
sostenuto, D major, two-four, theme for six bars to be
played on the second string. Rondo, Molto allegro, six-
eight, bright and spirited; the opening might have been
inspired by the Irish air "Garyone"—the lilt is so much
the same. The movement ends with a rapid descending
chromatic scale of three octaves. No. 4, Andante largo,
A minor, two-two, the opening bars of the theme for the
third string, declamatory, sad. Allegretto mottegiando,
two-four, light, tripping melody, to be delivered in a
spirit of banter. No. 5, Adagio amorosa, A major, two-
four, theme, Italian melody embellished, in thirds

throughout, with some semi-staccato bowing. Allegretto energicamente, two-four, a merry, quick-step movement of two eight-bar periods. The second part, in the tonic minor, has the theme divided equally for guitar and violin, in each strain. A coda of four bars, major, is added by way of close. In the arrangement for pianoforte, the violin has the theme throughout. No. 6, Andante innocentemente, E minor, four-four, a pathetic melody, simple, but touching. Allegro vivo e spiritoso, six-eight. One could imagine an Italian peasant singing this melody; it has all the characteristics of a folk-song. It is written throughout in double-notes, mostly thirds. The second part, in the minor, is in a different manner to the first part, which is repeated after it. The guitar accompaniments, with the exception named, are all in chords or arpeggios. The pianoforte part has more variety. It may be observed that the movements in two-four measure have much of the spirit of Haydn's Allegros.

Op. 4, Three Quartets for violin, viola, violoncello and guitar. These were once in the Circulating Music Libraries of the firms of Novello and Augener, but are no longer to be met with. I have failed to obtain copies elsewhere.

Op. 5, *Tre Quartetti a Violino, Viola, Chitarra e Violoncello. Composti e Dedicati Alle Amatrici Da Nicolò Paganini. Milano. Presso Gio. Ricordi.* By the courtesy of the firm of Novello, I have been enabled to examine this set, the title page of which I quote. The copy I examined is evidently of the original edition. Each quartet is in four movements. No. 1, Presto, D major, sixteen-eight, a peculiar signature, but apparently adopted by reason of the "figures" in quavers. This movement is very much in Rossini Overture form. Andante sotto voce e staccato, D minor, three-four, Canone a tre. The violin begins, the viola answers one bar later, an octave lower, and the violoncello follows in like manner. The guitar is silent. The Canon is kept up strictly to the end. The Trio—not in Canon—is in B flat major, and the guitar supports the strings with full chords. Tema con variazioni, Cantabile quasi Larghetto, D major, two-four, two strains of eight bars, the theme in each begun by the viola, and repeated by the violoncello. Three variations follow, the theme being allotted to each instrument in turn, the guitar included. Finale, Prestissimo, D major, three-eight, a brilliant, showy movement.

No. 2, Allegro, C major, four-four measure, in binary form, the subjects given to the violin and violoncello. Minuetto, Allegretto, A minor, three-four, with Trio in two sections, F major and D minor. The violin has the theme, the others accompany with chords. Cantabile, Larghetto, A major, six-eight, the melody, floridly embellished, for violin, the other instruments accompanying. Polacca, Quasi presto, C major, six-four. The violin has the chief melody, subordinate parts being given to the viola and violoncello. The guitar has full chords throughout.

No. 3, Allegro, D minor, four-four rhythm, Coda in D major, principal themes for the violin, the viola and violoncello taking up portions here and there with chords and arpeggios for the guitar. Allegro moderato, D minor, three-four, Canone a tre, theme for violin, answered by viola and violoncello at one bar interval, an octave below, as in No. 1. Guitar tacet. Tema Cantabile, Quasi adagio, B flat major, two-four. The movement consists of two periods, the theme for viola and violin alternately, in each. Variation I., florid, violoncello and violin in response; II., in G minor, more elaborate, theme for violoncello and violin, rapid arpeggios for guitar; III., in B flat major, theme for viola and violin, alternately, and finally for guitar. Polacchetta, Allegro con brio, D minor, three-four, a brilliant movement, with themes for the violin; the viola and violoncello share in the figurated passages, and the guitar has an accompaniment in chords and arpeggios.

Paganini is said to have repudiated this work, although according to Fétis, the quartets were published at Genoa under his very eyes. I should rather say that the Milan edition was the first, and perhaps the only one. Paganini's assertion was that some one had taken a few of his themes, and badly arranged them. Fétis further states that various pieces published before, and up to, 1851, must be considered as " commercial frauds." Some of them are named, and will be referred to in due course. The music of Op. 5 cannot be regarded as in any way great, but there are graceful melodies, and the movements in Canon form are ingeniously worked out.

Op. 6, *Premier Concerto (Mi Bémol), pour le violin avec accomp. de l'orchestrè.* This was the first of the posthumous works, published by the firm of Schott and Co., Paris, in

1851.   It is scored for two flutes, oboes, clarinets,
bassoon, double bassoon, two horns, trumpets, three
trombones, kettle drums, bass drum, cymbals, and the
usual quintet of strings.   The solo violin is tuned a semitone higher, and the part is in D, while the orchestra
plays in E flat.   Breitkopf and Härtel publish the
orchestral parts in the key of D.   There is an arrangement of the first movement, by August Wilhelmj, but
with that I have nothing to do here.   First movement,
Allegro maestoso, E flat, four-four.   The orchestral
exordium extends to ninety-four bars, six more than in
the introduction of Beethoven's Concerto.   The movement—so it may be termed—is symphonic in form, with
second subject in the dominant, and it is richly scored.
The exception I take to it is the persistent employment
of the cymbals with the bass drum.   There is a delightful
little touch in the canonic imitation for first violins and
violoncellos.   The solo has a principal theme scarcely
indicated in the introduction, and also several important
episodes.   The slow movement, Adagio, C minor, four-
four, was inspired, as already mentioned, by the Italian
tragedian, Demarini.   Paganini witnessed his performance
in a prison scene, where, after recapitulating his mis-
fortunes, he supplicated Providence to relieve him of the
burden of his life.   Paganini retired to rest still under
the influence of the emotions excited by the actor.   He
could not sleep : he rose and sought through his violin
a means of expression by which he could pour out the
feelings that consumed his soul.   Thus, genius tortures
and produces.   It must have been this movement in

which William Gardiner heard "tones more than human, which seemed to be wrung from the deepest anguish of a broken heart." Observe, especially, the recitative passages that close the movement. Finale, Rondo, Allegro spiritoso, E flat, two-four. This is the longest concerto movement known to me, running on to four hundred and eighty-three bars, but the "measure" is short. The concerto is not so long as that of Beethoven, the first and second movements containing fewer bars. It may be noted that in the first and last movements Paganini introduces harmonics, and passages in tenths, most probably for the first time in a concerto. In the slow movement there is no double stopping. The Cadenzas were improvised, and Paganini, like Beethoven, in his improvisations surpassed anything he ever committed to paper.

Op. 7, Concerto No. 2, in B minor. Allegro maestoso, B minor, twelve-eight. Adagio, D major, two-two. Rondo, Andantino allegretto moderato, B minor, six-eight. This is not so long as the first concerto by some two hundred bars, and is not so fine a work, but it is a piece worthy of being occasionally heard. In the principal theme of the Rondo occur the passages where the silver bell three times echoes the violin note—the top F sharp of the pianoforte keyboard. Failing the bell, the violinist produces the sound by an artificial harmonic. It is this Rondo that Liszt has included in his *Grosse Etüden von Paganini*. His treatment of Paganini must be briefly described. There are six "studies," the first a transcription of Paganini's Caprice, No. 6, Adagio, G

minor. To this Liszt adds a prefix, the arpeggio prelude
of No. 5. The Caprice itself is very literally copied, the
whole being an octave lower, and at first assigned to the
left hand alone. After the sixteenth bar the treatment
becomes more free, while the figuration is much the
same. The study ends with the arpeggio passage as at
the beginning. The second takes for subject No. 17,
Andante, E flat. Scarcely a note is omitted, but the
passages are placed higher or lower, and the runs given
to either hand. This is a marvel of ingenuity, forming a
most brilliant pianoforte solo. It is followed, as by a
second sonata movement, by the "Campanella" Rondo,
the two being intended to be performed in succession.
For this purpose the Rondo from the Concerto is transposed to G sharp minor, the closing E flat of the previous
movement changing enharmonically to D sharp.

The first exposition of the subject follows Paganini
very closely, but in the development and further progress
of the movement Liszt follows his own bent, repeating
the principal theme again and again with ever varying
treatment. This is a piece for the *virtuoso*, and one of the
most showy in the pianist's repertory. The fourth study
is an extremely clever transcription of the Caprice No. 1,
Andante, E major. Not a note of Paganini's piece is
left out, and the arpeggios are ingeniously set out for
interwoven fingering, causing the performance to be
something to look at as well as to hear. It is nearly all
cross-handed work. The fifth study is an arrangement of
the Caprice No. 9, Allegretto, E major. On paper it
appears easier than the setting by Schumann, but it is

more difficult to play. Here, again, the phrases are divided for both hands. The *glissando* passages in sixths are impossible on modern instruments. The sixth and last study, on the Caprice, No. 24, Tema, con variazioni, A minor, is the most ingenious of all. The theme is simply harmonised at first, then used as a counterpoint to the arpeggios in the first variation. The next is more simply treated, and in the third variation Paganini's theme forms the bass upon which the figuration of the initial motive is superposed. To the end Liszt shows what possibilities in keyboard execution were latent in Paganini's violin figures; and if the latter had written only these Capriccios he would survive as the cause of the most original inventions in pianoforte technique that have yet seen the light.

Op. 8, *Le Streghe.* Variations on the "Witches' Dance," theme from the Ballet, " Le Nozze di Benevento," by Vigano, music by Süssmayer. It has already been stated that Paganini witnessed a performance of this ballet, at La Scala, Milan, in 1813. He took the theme from a fantastic scene where the witches appear. In his London programmes Paganini thus described the piece; "Variations on the Country Dance Della Streghe alla Noce di Benevento (or the comic dances of the Witches under the walnut tree of Benevento), composed and performed by Signor Paganini." The piece is in the key of E flat, and the violin is to be tuned a semitone higher, the soloist playing in D. There is an orchestral prelude of eighteen bars, Maestoso, followed by a solo, Larghetto, a beautiful Italian melody, embellished, in two short strains. The theme is simply set forth, and the variations serve for the display of bravura playing with pizzicato and harmonics in the second movement, fourth string melody, and double harmonics in the third, and with the Finale resembling a Galopade. Orchestral parts are published, as well as the arrangement with pianoforte.

Op. 9, Variations on "God save the King." Théme, Andante, G major, with Six Variations. One principal feature is the intermingling of left hand staccato with bowed notes. At the close there are sustained open notes on the G and D strings, bowed, with double pizzicato, in sixths, above.

Op. 10, Variations on "The Carnival of Venice." For this the violin is tuned a semitone higher, the solo being played in A, and the accompaniment in B flat. The theme is a popular Venetian air, "O Mamma!" Paganini heard it when in Venice in 1816, but whether he then composed the variations is not certain. It was not long, however, before Paganini made the air a favourite everywhere he went, and it is to him the melody owes its world-wide popularity. The composer of the air remains unknown. Joseph Ghys published, at Paris and Berlin, what purported to be Paganini's variations; Ernst and Sivori played versions more or less exactly in accordance with the original; but the text was finally settled by the publication of the piece in 1851. There are twenty variations. The 9th and 14th are for the fourth string; the 11th has alternate bowed and pizzicato notes; the 15th and 18th are pizzicato throughout; the 19th is in tenths and thirds; and the piece ends with a short brilliant coda.

Op. 11, *Moto Perpetuo*. Allegro vivace, C major. Fétis terms this piece a movement from a Sonata for violin and orchestra. It is in the repertory for all violinists, and its running passages of staccato semi-quavers need no description.

Op. 12, Introduction and Variations on the air " Non più mesta accanto al fuoco." The theme is from Rossini's opera " La Cenerentola " (Cinderella), produced at Rome during the Carnival season of 1817, and forms the concluding number of the work. Paganini again directs the violin to be tuned a semitone higher, writing the solo part in D, and the accompaniment in E flat. The Introduction, Adagio Cantabile, is another example of Paganini's pure Italian style of melody. The theme seems to have appealed to him—doubtless he witnessed the *première* of the opera—for the variations have a spontaneity and brilliance of their own. There are four variations, and a Finale full of dashing *bravura*.

Op. 13, Introduction and Variations on the air " Di tanti palpiti," from Rossini's first serious opera, " Tancredi," produced at Venice in 1813. Rossini is said to have taken the theme from a Greek Litany he heard sung in a church on one of the Islets of the Laguna, near Venice. A Signora Righetti, a singer, writing in 1823 (?), stated that there was no truth in the assertion. Be that as it may, " Di tanti palpiti " made the opera, and Paganini's variations extended its popularity. The intro-duction is an elaborate movement, the violin tuned a semitone higher, and the part written in A, with accompaniment in B flat.   There are three variations, the second being almost throughout in harmonics, single and double, and excessively difficult.   This piece is very rarely played.

Op. 14, Sixty Studies in Variation form, on the air known at Genoa as " Barucabà," for violin alone.   This is one of the composer's latest works, and was written at Genoa in February 1835, and dedicated to Paganini's friend the Advocate, L. G. Germi.   The theme is short, in simple ternary form, the opening sentence of four bars being repeated after the middle period of eight bars.   The theme is in A major, Maestoso.   The variations are studies upon various species of difficulties, and a special feature is the order of keys.   Of the fifteen possible major keys, Paganini employs thirteen, and he is quite modern in the way in which he causes the one to succeed the other.   Thus the second variation is in D, the third in B flat, the fourth in F sharp, and the fifth in D—in each case the drop of a major third or its enharmonic equivalent.   Then he starts a new series, from D to B, thence to G, E, C, A flat, F, D flat, back to A.   In 1835 such a sequence was very uncommon; even Beethoven, in his Variations, only has one such, in the Variations in F, Op. 34.   The Variation form is again in full vogue; at this distance we can afford to be just in our estimate of Paganini's achievements.   He was not a Beethoven, but his Variations are not to be despised.

WORKS WITHOUT OPUS NUMBER.

Sonata in A major.   As published in the collection of

posthumous compositions, this Sonata is for violin, with pianoforte accompaniment. The piece consists of an Introduction, Theme, Three Variations and Coda, the term "Sonata" being employed quite in its primitive sense:—a piece to be played. The Introduction is only eight bars in length, ending with a short cadenza leading to the theme, Andantino, A major, two-four measure. The first part consists of two four-bar phrases, repeated; the second has a phrase extended, by a Codetta, to six bars, and ends with a repetition of the first phrase, with close in A. The first variation has a more florid version, in triplets, of the melody; the second begins with a simple form of the theme for the fourth string, and introduces harmonics; the third is a bravura movement, chiefly for staccato bowing in demisemiquaver passages. The coda, termed Finale, is made up of cadences, on a tonic pedal for eight bars. The accompaniment is easy. Messrs. Schott also publish the Sonata for violin, with accompaniment of violin and violoncello, very easy parts for these last.

Variazioni di bravura sopra Temi del Mosè di G. Rossini, per Violino sulla quarta corda, di Nicolo Paganini. This was originally for violin and orchestra. Berlioz has a reference to this piece, in which he states that Paganini employed the bass-drum with better effect than did Rossini himself in the accompaniment to the prayer, "Del tuo stellato soglio." Paganini placed the stroke of the drum on the syncopated beat to which the verbal accent was assigned, whereas Rossini gave the drum stroke on the first beat of the bar. Some one, compli-

menting Paganini upon his composition, added ; " It must
be confessed that Rossini furnished you a very beautiful
theme." " That's very true," replied Paganini, " but he
didn't invent my bang of the big drum." It is said that
in this piece Paganini produced a tone that dominated the
whole orchestra even in fortissimo passages.

The firm of Ricordi publish an arrangement, for string
quintet, and for pianforte accompaniment. The G string
of the solo violin is raised to B flat, and the Adagio is
played in C minor and major, while the accompaniment
is in E flat minor and major. The strain in the minor
key is played three times. The second time, the first
eight bars are to be played an octave higher then the first
time ; the third in harmonics. The Introductory Adagio
is the celebrated Prayer. Then follows a Tema, Tempo
alla Marcia, E flat, four-four, the violin part in C. This
is a different theme, and appears to be a paraphrase of
part of the March and Chorus (in the Oratorio), " Hail,
happy day ! " There are three variations, and a short
coda. Harmonics are sparingly introduced. Rossini's
opera, " Mosè in Egitto," was produced at Naples in 1818,
and was remodelled by the composer some years later,
for performance at the Grand Opera, Paris (1827). It
is not known when Paganini wrote his variations, but his
themes were most probably taken from the first version
of the opera.

*Variazioni di Bravura per Violino sopra un tema originale
con accompagnamento di Piano o Chitarra.* The theme is
that of the Twenty-fourth Caprice, from Op. 1, and the
variations are the same, only the notation of the eighth is

different. The accompaniment, for either guiter or pianoforte, is extremely simple. There is a short interlude (called *Tutti* in Ricordi's edition) of six bars to be played between the variations.

Introduzione e Variazioni sul Tema nel cor più mi sento per Violino solo di Nicolò Paganini. So runs the title in the edition published by Ricordi and Co. The theme is the duet in Paisiello's opera, *La Molinara,* which Beethoven also took as a subject for variations (in 1795). Ricordi's publication agrees in every particular with the version to be found in Guhr's treatise on Paganini's "Art of Playing the Violin," published in 1831—preface dated Frankfurt, November, 1829. Guhr* heard Paganini many times, closely watched his playing, and frequently conversed with him on the subject. This piece was written from memory, and is certainly a great accomplishment; but it can scarcely be regarded as an authentic version. The introduction is brilliant, the theme, Andante, G major, six-eight measure, is profusely ornamented, and each of the seven variations—No. 6 is in G minor, the others in G major—has some special form of virtuosity. In the third there are double shakes in harmonics, which Guhr explains. The last is in widespread ascending and descending arpeggios throughout. The theme and third variation are written on two staves, one for bowed melody, the other for left hand pizzicato.

That Paganini did not always play the piece in the

---

* Carl F. W. Guhr, born at Militsch, Silesia, October 30th, 1787, violinist, pianist and composer, became Director of the Museum Concerts and Conductor of the Opera at Frankfort-on-the-Main, in which city he died July 22nd, 1848.

form in which Guhr wrote it down, is proved by the
existence of another manuscript, which is, perhaps, very
little known. It was written by the late Mrs. Tom
Taylor, who gave it to Mr. Alfred Burnett many years
ago, and that gentleman has kindly permitted me to
examine it. For this the violin is tuned a whole tone
higher. The Introduction is altogether different, and the
theme much less floridly embellished. The first variation
corresponds to Guhr's No. 2, but the harmonics are not
quite the same. In this the melody floats above
tremolando chords. The second, in outline, resembles
Guhr's No. 4, but whereas the latter has alternate
natural notes and harmonics, Mrs. Taylor gives alternations of detached bowed notes and pizzicati. The
third is like Guhr's No. 3, in that it has short figures in
double notes, alternately for fundamental and harmonic
sounds. Guhr's variation consists of twenty-five bars;
Mrs. Taylor's of thirty-one, there being a short cadenza.
The fourth resembles Guhr's No. 7 in the wide-spread
arpeggios, but the harmonics are differently distributed,
and the coda is not the same as in Guhr.*

In the Imperial Library, Berlin, there is a manuscript
by Paganini, inscribed "Capriccio a Violino Solo di
Nicolo Paganini In cor più non mi sento," in which the
embellished theme differs from both those already des-

* Mrs. Tom Taylor (*née* Laura Wilson Barker) was a fine
musician, a composer, and almost phenomenal performer on the
pianoforte and the violin. She played with both Spohr and
Paganini, and took down this set of variations after hearing
Paganini play them twice. She died at Coleshill, Bucks, May 22nd,
1905, at the advanced age of eighty-six.

cribed. The first page is reproduced in facsimile in Paul Stoeving's "Story of the Violin," p. 213. Then there is an autograph copy in the British Museum with this inscription: " In cuor più non mi sento, Thema con variazioni per Violino, con Accompagnementi di Violino e Violoncello Composta da Niccolo Paganini." The piece consists of an Introduction, Theme and four Variations, and, so far, agrees with Mrs. Taylor's copy. Finally, Paganini played the piece with the orchestra, as will be seen from this extract from a programme : " Prelude and Variations on the Tema, ' Nel cor più non missento,' with orchestral accompaniment, by Signor Paganini." This was played at the concert of June 27th, 1831, at the King's Theatre, and the programme from which this extract is taken is in possession of Mr. Richard Harrison, of Brighton, who most obligingly copied it for me.

Duo pour le violon seul. This begins with an Adagio, C major, three-four measure, with a melody for the bow, and left hand pizzicato accompaniment. A short Allegro molto follows, in square time, the pizzicato accompaniment being chiefly in double notes, with occasional chromatic harmonics. This little piece must have been on sale in London a year before Paganini arrived, for the following anecdote was in print in May, 1830. "A few days since, a footman went into Mori's music shop to buy a fiddle string. While he was making his choice a gentleman entered the shop, and began to examine various compositions for the violin. Among the rest he found Paganini's celebrated *Merveille—duo pour un seul Violon* and, perceiving the difficulties in which it abounded,

PLATE 25. (See Appendix.)

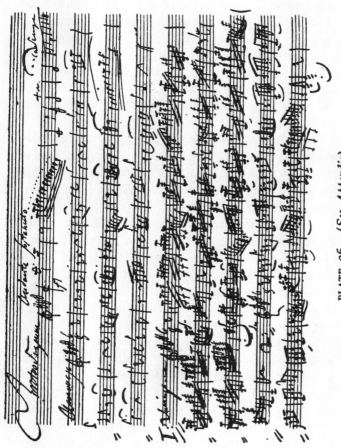

PLATE 26. (See Appendix).

asked the shopman if he thought that Mori himself
could play it. The young man, a little perplexed and
unwilling to imply that his master's powers had any limits,
at length replied, that he had no doubt he could perform
it, provided he practised it for a week. Upon which the
footman, who stood intent upon the conversation, broke
in on the discourse and swore that Mori could do no
such thing, for that he himself had been practising the
piece for three weeks and could not play it yet."

Trois Airs Variés pour le Violon, pour être exécutes
sur la Quatrieme Corda seulement, avec accompagnement
de Piano par Gustavo Carulli. Fétis says these are
merely souvenirs arranged by the author of the accompaniments.* Antonio Minasi includes them in the
lists of works performed by Paganini in England. The
fourth string is to be raised to A, for all three. The first
is in C, with two easy variations; the second, in G,
resembles a folk song, and has three variations; the third,
in C, also has three variations. The first two are
marked Andante; the third, Andantino. The accompaniments are of the easiest song kind.

Le Charme de Padua, Divertimento pour Violon et
Piano concertant, composé par Nicolo Paganini. This
piece was published in London before the date of
Paganini's first concert, and possibly before the arrival of
that artist in England. It was issued by a firm of repute,
Wessel and Stodar, who were the first publishers in
England of the works of Chopin. The music was

---

* Gustavo Carulli was the son of the celebrated guitarrist,
Ferdinando Carulli, and was born at Leghorn in 1801.

reviewed in *The Harmonicon,* June 1831, the notice concluding thus: " It perhaps is a bagatelle on which he (Paganini) has bestowed little time and less thought. It certainly is a flimsy affair, and might have been produced by the dullest and most mechanical *repieno* in the band of a suburb (*sic*) theatre." The piece consists of a Larghetto and Presto, in C major, the slow introduction being in six-eight rhythm, the Presto in six-four. There is one principal theme in the first part, given out by the violin and repeated by the pianoforte, a simple melody, with embellishments. The Presto is in Rondo form, with leading theme for pianoforte, continued by violin, and relieved by an episode contrasted in character. The music is not great, but unprejudiced musicians will scarcely endorse the captious remarks of the reviewer. The firm of Edwin Ashdown (successor to Wessel) publish the composition, also a version by S. Godbé for viola and pianoforte. In this the themes are written an octave lower, and modifications occur in double-stops, and so forth, to suit the viola. There is likewise an arrangement for flute and pianoforte, by J. Sedlazek. It is not stated by whom the pianoforte part was written, but it is very well done, and is not a mere accompaniment.

WORKS UNPUBLISHED, OR LOST.

Concerto in D minor. Fétis terms this a magnificent concerto; it was performed by Paganini at the first concert he gave in Paris, March 25th, 1831, and that seems to be all that is known about the piece. Concerto in E minor. This was in three movements; Allegro

maestoso; Adagio flebile, con sentimento; Rondo, Andantino Gàjo, "with a triangle accompaniment." It was
played by Paganini at the King's Theatre, June 13th,
1831. Concerto in E major. The three movements of
this piece were; Allegro Marziale; Cantabile Spianato;
and Polacca brillante. Paganini played this concerto at
his concert, July 4th, 1831. Concerto in two movements.
This was a medley. The one movement, Cantabile
a doppie corde, was by Paganini; the other, Rondo
scherzoso, by Rodolphe Kreutzer. Played, August 17th,
1831.

Four Concertos, of which the instrumentation was not
written. Of these nothing seems now to be known.
Fétis says that the last of the four was composed at Nice
a short time before the death of Paganini.

Concerto for bassoon, with string trio accompaniment.
This was discovered at Stockholm in 1890, and the
manuscript was said to be in the composer's hand-writing.
The announcement of the discovery will be found in
The Musical Times, of November, 1890, page 681. I have
found no further reference to the subject.

Nine Quartets for Violin, Viola, Violoncello and Guitar.
These are in the list drawn up by Constabile as being
among the manuscripts preserved by the son of the
composer. It is impossible now to say where these
manuscripts are; the first three seem completely lost.
A copy, probably unique, of the Quartets, Nos. 10 to 15,
is among the treasures in the possession of Mr. Alfred
Burnett, and by his kindness I am enabled to give a
description of the music. Five of the Quartets, Nos. 10

to 14, were composed and dedicated "Al suo Amico Il
Sig. Avvocato Luigi Guglièlmo Germi." No. 14 was
composed "expressly" for that friend. The Quartets
dedicated to Germi might be designated "house music,"
for though they are difficult, they do not seem to have
been written for the "great public." They contain the
most lovely music Paganini ever penned. If only the
guitar were once more in fashion, these pieces might be
heard, and I feel certain they would charm lovers of
pure melody.* But this is to anticipate.

Quartet, No. 10, in A major, in four movements (as
indeed are five out of the six). Allegro, A major, four-
four rhythm, in free sonata form, with first and second
subject—both lyrical—middle modulatory section, and
recapitulation. The violin has the melody, the other instruments accompanying. Minuetto Scherzo, Allegretto,
A major, three-four measure, with first short strain on a
figure in triplets. Trio in D major, Cantabile theme for
violin, doubled by the viola in the octave below. Adagio
Cantabile, D major, two-four rhythm. A melody that
might be signed Haydn or Mozart, but embellished with
a grace peculiar to Italian art. Here the violin is the solo
instrument, the others supporting with rich harmonies,
the 'cello emphasising the rhythm with frequent pizzicato
notes. Rondo Andantino con brio, A major, two-four
measure, a bright, sparkling principal theme, staccato,
with contrasting episodes, one in D, with fourth string

* They were performed at the private quartet concerts given by
Mr. Burnett in the Art Club, Blackheath, from about the year
1893 onward.

phrases, also with brilliant passages in thirds for the violin, which again has all the thematic work. This is a well developed movement.

Quartet, No. 11, in B major. For this the guitar is tuned a tone higher, the *capo tasto* raising the E strings to F sharp, and the guitar part is written in the open key of A. The first movement, Allegro moderato, B major, four-four rhythm is free in form, with repeat of the first part. The thematic material is assigned chiefly to the violin, but in the second part there is an episode, a sort of folk-tune, given to the violoncello. Minuetto, Allegretto, B major, three-four, with Trio in G major. The melodies are fresh, and move step-wise, very much like those in the Minuet of Beethoven's first Symphony. They are in scale formation, up and down, and there is only one skip of a third in the first sixteen bars. Again the violin takes all the themes. Larghetto con passione, F sharp minor, six-eight measure, a Lament, a fine expressive theme, opening nobly, but with the elevated style not maintained throughout. The viola and violoncello parts are in keeping with the pathetic feeling of the movement, but the rhythmic figure of the guitar part detracts from its dignity. Polacca, Andantino mosso, B major, three-four measure, a well-written movement, with three clearly defined subjects, two of which are taken up by the viola and violoncello. The violin part in this quartet is brilliant, but not particularly difficult; there is no double-stopping, excepting in chords of accompaniment.

Quartet, No. 12, in A minor. This number is in three

movements only. The first, Allegro giusto, A minor, four-four rhythm, is quite orchestral in character, and opens with a theme of symphonic breadth. There is science displayed in the development of this movement. In the first part the second subject is in C major, and in the recapitulation in A major. The slow movement, Adagio tenuto, con precisione, C major, three-four measure, has at first a very broad and declamatory theme for the violin. The writing becomes very elaborate, and the rhythmic figuration complex, passages with four and five-stroke notes occurring. The Finale, Minuetto, Allegretto mosso, is a fully developed movement quite in sonata form, with first part repeated. The exposition has a first subject of two extended members, the second in the major mode. The second subject, in E, is well contrasted. There is a long working out section, with episodial matter, and the recapitulation is very happily led up to. The music has a lilt that is irresistible, and the writing is interesting for each instrument.

Quartet, No. 13, in F. The first movement, Allegro con brio, F major, four-four time, opens with a theme of a declamatory type, and the expression is dramatic. The second subject in C, is in the style of the Italian *aria*, concluding with the lively *Cabaletta* strain. A short *Coda* ends the first part. In the working out section there is an important episodial theme for the violoncello, and in the recapitulation the second subject, now in F, is allotted to the viola, the violin taking up the *Cabaletta*. Both parts are marked for repetition. Minuetto, Allegretto, F major, three-four measure. The violin has the theme of the first strain of eight bars repeated; the violoncello responds with the subject of the next strain of twenty-five bars, one phrase lengthened to five bars. The Trio in B flat has a tripping theme for the viola, legato and staccato bowing in the same "figure." Later the phrases are broken into dialogue for violin and viola. In the Minuet the guitar has a "second" to the violin melody. Larghetto tenuto, con anima, D flat major, six-eight rhythm, a broad, cantabile theme for the violin, with spare embellishment. The movement must be slow, for there are arpeggios of eight notes to the quaver beat in the guitar part. Finale, Prestissimo, F major, two-two measure. The theme for the violin resembles very much some of those merry "tributary" motives found in Mozart's symphonies towards the close of the first part of a movement—the "Jupiter," first movement for instance. The second subject affords contrast. The whole is most spirited and light-hearted. Paganini must have been in a happy mood when he wrote this quartet.

Quartet, No. 14, in A major. The first movement, Allegro maestoso, A major, four-four measure, is very brilliant, opening with a theme in which arpeggio and scale figures abound. This closes in B, and the second subject begins in E. Here occurs some very free chromatic writing, suggestive of Richard Strauss, as, for instance, D sharp for violoncello against E flat for guitar and viola; and C natural opposed to B sharp. But it is a mere matter of spelling. The first part ends in E, and is marked for repetition. Then, with a single prefatory chord of E minor, the working out section begins in C, with a new motive, which passes through a number of keys, the primary returning with the second subject. Minuetto, Scherzo affettuoso, A major, three-four. The subject is based on a three-note figure, giving, by cross accents, to the four-bar phrase the effect of a six-bar phrase in duple measure—Tempo rubato. The Trio, in D, has a theme in triple measure, but the middle sentence has the displaced accents of the Minuet. Largo, con sentimento, G flat major, four-four measure. For this the pitch of the guitar is raised a tone, and the part written in E major. The movement is in song form, the melody opening in stately fashion, but the writing soon becomes florid. At the second entry the theme begins in A major, the return to G flat being ingeniously effected. There are some rapid pizzicato passages for the violoncello. Finale, Allegro vivace, A major, four-four rhythm. This is a moto perpetuo, sempre staccato, for the violin. The theme is quite unlike that of the movement known as Op. 11. After the exposition of the subject, the violin has figure-playing of an easy kind, while the violoncello has a Cantabile theme. This recurs, and snatches of it are heard in the brief coda. The other instruments merely accompany. This quartet has distinct character.

Quartet, No. 15. The title simply runs : "Composto da Nicola Paganini," without any dedication. Note the copyist's spelling of the Christian name. In the first movement, Maestoso, A minor, four-four measure, the first subject is given out by the viola. It begins with a mournful, somewhat stern motive, bold, and with an embellished subordinate theme. The second subject, also assigned to the viola, is an impassioned lyrical theme in C major. In the working out section, the violin takes the first subject, and joins the violoncello in an episodial theme, the viola contributing a florid counterpoint. There are modifications in the recapitulation, but the viola again has the second subject now in the tonic major. The guitar is busy throughout the movement, with full chords and extended arpeggios. Minuetto a Canone, Andantino, A major, three-four measure. The Canon is confined to the violin and viola, the latter starting with a theme in short, detached figures, the violin following, an octave higher, one beat later. Guitar and violoncello give supporting harmonies. In the Trio, in D major, the melody is given to the guitar, with a pizzicato accompaniment for the other instruments. At the seventeenth bar, there are again four bars of canon, this time in the unison, staccato bowing. The Minuet, abbreviated, is then repeated. The canon is not continuous, a cadence occurring at the end of each eight bars. Next comes an Interlude, Recitative, Andante sostenuto, con sentimento, D major. This is for the viola, and extends to twenty-one bars, the expression being dramatic. The other instruments have a rather elaborate accompaniment. The slow movement immediately ensues, Adagio Cantabile, D major, two-four rhythm. The viola has the melody, in the form of the Italian aria, embellished with prima donna fioriture. The movement is short, only running to forty-six bars. Rondo, Allegretto, A minor, two-four. The leading theme, marked by syncopations, is given to the viola, the violin joining in the repetition. The tonality is constantly changing from the minor to the major and back again. There is a new theme in the middle section, and some elaboration before the first subject returns. The close is abrupt. The viola has the chief part in this quartet, which is quite different to the others.

I have only a few notes concerning some of the works yet to be considered. Dramatic Sonata, "The Storm," for violin and orchestra. This was evidently a piece of programme music, for it was thus described:—Part I., the approach of the storm; II., the commencement of the tempest; III., the prayer; IV., the fury of the sea; V., the hurricane; VI., the tumult at its height; VII., the stilling of the tempest; VIII., an outburst of the most lively joy. It was played at Paganini's third and last concert at Prague, December 20th, 1828, and one account refers to it as a "dramatic sonata for a full orchestra, with analogous embellishments and solos and variations, by Paganini on the fourth string."*

"Sonata Militaire," in G, for the fourth string, theme, the air "Non più andrai," from Mozart's opera "Le Nozze di Figaro." This piece was composed expressly for the second of the two concerts Paganini gave in Genoa in 1824, when the young singer, Antonia Bianchi, made her début. The Sonata was played by Paganini at his first concert in London. All traces of it appear to have been lost.

"Napoleon Sonata," for the fourth string. Paganini

---

* *The Quarterly Musical Magazine and Review*, Vol. X., p. 205.

gave an account of the origin of this piece to his friend,
Julius Schottky, and to what has already been related in
connection therewith may now be added the further
statement he made.   Paganini sang to his friend the
first movement of this Sonata " in an animated though
feeble tone," and said that Rossini transferred the theme
into one of his earlier operas.   It would be interesting to
know the opera in question, but the early works of Rossini
would be searched in vain without the clue afforded by
the Sonata, which appears to have vanished completely.

" Sonata Maestosa Sentimentale," with variations on
a theme by Haydn, for the fourth string.   It is probable
that the theme for these variations was the well-known
Emperor's Hymn, and that this Sonata was performed
by Paganini before the Austrian Court in 1828.

Sonata with variations on a theme from the opera
" L'Amor Marinaro."   Nothing is now known of this
Sonata, nor of the particular theme chosen from the
opera.   " L'Amor Marinaro " (the Corsair in Love) was
one of the early productions of Joseph Weigl, being
written in 1798.   An opera buffa, it was distinguished by
natural charm, freshness of colouring and beauty of
melody, and to the latter quality Paganini's choice of it
must doubtless be attributed.

" Chant of the Monks of the Monastery of St. Bernard."
This was the title given to a piece in the programme of
a concert at Covent Garden Theatre.   It was performed
on a darkened stage and the solemn character of its
music was emphasized by a beautiful scene representing
a monastery with stained glass windows.   The introduc-

tion, a movement of some length of the basses in unison, was followed by a chant "of lovely harmonies, performed in harmonics (I believe, on the fourth strings) in combination with the wood instruments." Minasi, who gives this account of the piece, states that he believes it to be merely the second movement of the Concerto in B minor, Op. 7.

Cantabile for two strings. This piece was performed at the King's Theatre, on June 13th, 1831. Possibly it was the same as the musical fantasia already referred to as played at Lucca under the title of "A Love Scene." Of the remaining pieces, except the one mentioned below, nothing seems now to be known save the names.

The one exception is the piece entitled "The Vagaries of a Farmyard," which contained a wonderful series of imitations of farmyard sounds. In this connection the following anecdote, illustrating Paganini's extraordinary power of portraying curious sounds on his violin, may be worth repeating. One fine night, when staying at a little inn just outside Frankfort, he was sitting at his window lost in the contemplation of the glorious heavens. The striking of a clock broke through his reverie and called back to his mind an occurrence of which he had but recently been an ear-witness. He seized his violin, and there arose on the stillness of the night the moans and cries of a mother and her new-born babe. The landlord of the inn, awakened by the unusual sounds and wondering how such visitors had found their way into his house without his knowledge, called his son and hastened to the

room whence the plaintive cries proceeded ; and he found
Paganini, too deep in thought to perceive his entrance,
making his violin bring forth these human sounds.   It
is stated of Paganini that he was wont to produce his
animal cries under the stress of special excitement or
during an access of fever, and that with his farmyard
piece he electrified the audience at one of the last of his
concerts in London.

Plate 27.—See Appendix.

MEDAL STRUCK IN PAGANINI'S HONOUR IN 1831.

CHAPTER XII.

THIS may have been the concert at which, according to a lithograph,* Paganini received " the homage of five thousand persons after having pocketed £2,000 for two hours' performance." While the great world showed their appreciation of his playing in this way, and Royal patrons delighted to invest him with noble orders, the more humble admirers of Paganini caused medals to be struck in his honour. One of these, a tribute from the city of Vienna, has already been referred to; another very fine medal, struck in Paris during Paganini's first visit there in 1831 is reproduced here. The inscription round Paganini's head fills one with a strangely ironical feeling, when one remembers that the fame of Paganini did but survive to lead to the homage of exhumation.

True, the world has remembered him sufficiently to place memorial tablets on the houses where he was born and died. Fifty years after his death a tablet was affixed to the house wherein he breathed his last, and at the centenary celebration of his birth the following inscription was placed on the house wherein he first saw the light: " A great honour fell to the lot of this modest house, in which, on the 27th October, 1782, Nicolo Paganini, unsurpassed in the divine art of tone, was born, to the glory of Genoa and to the delight of the

---

* Reproduced on page 144.

world." At present one may enquire in vain of most
Genoese people as to the position of Paganini's birthplace, and chance alone will direct one, who trusts to
them for the information, to the slum quarter and the
narrow street where the building stands. Difficult though
it may be, however, to find this spot, it is an easy task to
find the Palazzo Municipale where reposes the famous
Guarnerius violin of Paganini.

This superb instrument, bequeathed to the city of
Genoa by Paganini himself, has been most carefully
preserved by the civic authorities. It has only twice
been heard in public—once at the 1882 celebrations—
since Paganini's death, and on both occasions it was
played by his favourite pupil Sivori. It was carefully
examined and photographed by Mr. Edward Heron-
Allen in 1885, and a very interesting account was given
by him* of the manner in which the violin was worn
away by Paganini's peculiar method of playing. After
describing its general condition he says, " The patch by
the side of the tailpiece and the large wear on the back
tell of the force with which he held the instrument in
those high and pizzicato passages, which account for the
long groove down the side of the fingerboard and the
broad patch at the side of the neck, on the table of
the instrument. The wearing away of the edges in
the curves of the instrument bear a striking testimony
to the force with which he sawed the gut in his bravura
passages on the first and fourth strings." In the same
glass case as the violin is placed the medal presented to

---

* *The Musical Times*, May 1st, 1886.

Paganini by the Decurional Council of Genoa in 1834. On the reverse it bears this inscription :—

Nic. Paganino, Fidicini, cui nemo par
fuit civique bene mecrenti A.D. MDCCCXXXIIII.

Such outward honours as the world gives to its dead have indeed been offered to the memory of Paganini; but it is doubtful whether the higher honour of a frank recognition by the musical world of the work that he did for it, has ever been his. Unlike the great composer the instrumentalist leaves behind him no visible proof of the part he has played in the development of his art. And the world has easily forgotten that from the day of Paganini not only was the violin transformed into a new instrument, not only were its capabilities, previously undreamt of, newly revealed, but also in other branches of musical art, in orchestral music especially, a fresh field was opened up before the composer. It is scarcely too much to say that the scores of Tchaikovsky and Richard Strauss could not have been written, had Paganini never lived. We do not desire to see another Paganini, so complete a slave to his instrument, albeit its master; we do not desire to see another such life, with bodily health and moral vigour sacrificed to so absorbing a devotion to one single end. We would fain believe that Nicolo' Paganini did not live in vain, that like a real artist he had and fulfilled his mission, that the evil he did died with him and that the good lives on to benefit the world.

THE END.

APPENDIX.

NOTES ON THE ILLUSTRATIONS IN THIS VOLUME.

Plate 1—Frontispiece.

Portrait of NICOLÒ PAGANINI, by Maurin, a French Artist. Free from caricature, it is probably the most authentic picture of the great virtuoso. It appeared in the seventh volume of the " Revue Musicale."

Plate 2—Facing page 4.

THE BIRTHPLACE OF THE CELEBRATED PAGANINI in the Passo di Gatto Moro, Genoa, Italy. The house is in a squalid neighbourhood—a dirty, narrow alley now occupied by the poorest of the city. Probably no worse than at the time of Paganini's birth. There is a tablet which reads as follows :—

Alta ventura sortita ad umile luogo
in questa casa
il giorno XXVII di Ottobre dell' anno
MDCCLXXXII
Nacque
a decoro di Genova a delizia del mondo
Nicolò Paganini
nella divina arte dei suoni insuperato maestro.

The date 1782 given here confirms the latest research that Paganini was born in that year and not in 1784 so usually quoted.

Plate 3—Facing page 14.

PAGANINI'S VIOLIN, BOW, CASE, ETC., in the Municipal Museum at Genoa. This is the celebrated Joseph Guarnerius on which the great virtuoso invariably performed. The instrument is under a glass shade, and with other relics of Paganini, preserved in a strong safe. It is stated that £5,000 has, in vain, been offered for the violin.

Plate 4—Facing page 20.

THIS IS ANOTHER CARICATURE—Paganini performing on a tight rope—under which is printed " Exercices sur une seule corde,"—in reference to his one string solos. This was published by Mori and Lavenu, London, circa 1831.

Plate 5— Facing page 40.

This is, we believe, from a contemporary German picture.

Plate 6—Facing page 50.

This humorous picture is on the title-page of a comic song, "The wonderful Paganini, or London fiddling mad." The poetry by W. T. Moncrieff, Esq., and the melody by one of the first composers of the day! London, published by Leoni Lee, circa 1831. The ' poetry " is not of a classical standard.

"What a hubbub! what a fuss! all London sure are frantic Sirs,
    The Prince of Fiddlers has arriv'd, great Paganini has come.
So wonderful, exorbitant, so frightful, so romantic, Sirs, the
    world of Music at his mighty presence are struck dumb.
So firm his touch, so fine his stop, everyone must own his sway,
Great King King of Catgut! Agitato! presto! Who but he Sirs,
    Mori, Spagnoletti, now must second fiddle play, Sirs—
Glory be to Tweedle dum! Success to Tweedle dee! Sirs—

Such golden sounds, he from one string can draw, no sum can
  pay him, Sirs,
Germany, France, Italy, combined his fame to puff
The prices must be doubled, all the world crowd to survey
  him, Sirs,
Four thousand pounds a night to pay him is not half enough,
Sixpences, none, after this, must dare call fiddlers' money Sirs,
Thousands, tens of thousands, must the wondrous man reward,
               etc., etc.,
        and so on for five verses !

Plate 7—Facing page 54.

SIGR. PAGANINI. During one of his performances at
the King's Theatre, June, 1831. From a contemporary
lithograph of the celebrated sketch by D. Maclise, R.A.,
now in the Foster Collection, South Kensington Museum.
In the background are J. B. Cramer, Lindley, Dragonetti,
Mori, etc. This is, perhaps, the most interesting print of
the great violinist. It was published on July 12th, 1831,
by W. Spooner, 259, Regent Street, London.

Plate 8—Facing page 60.

Reproduction of the celebrated Statuette (caricature),
by Dainton.

Plate 9—Facing page 66.

PAGANINI WITH THE VIOLIN, Rossini at the pianoforte
and the celebrated prima-donna Pasta. (Jos. McGuire,
delt., printed by Englemann & Co.), circa 1832.

Plate 10—Facing page 76.

A COPY OF THE ORIGINAL OIL PAINTING OF
PAGANINI in the Municipal Museum at Genoa. The face
full of intellect, shows the ravages of the disease which
was so soon to terminate his existence.

Plate 11—Facing page 80.

THE HOUSE AT NICE IN WHICH PAGANINI DIED on the 27th May, 1840. It was formerly the residence of the Count de Sessol. The lower part has been converted into shops.

Plate 12—Facing page 80.

THE TABLET, with inscription, fixed on the front of the house, Rue de la Prefecture, Nice, France.

Plate 13—Facing page 84.

THE TOMB OF PAGANINI AT PARMA. Neither religious nor political martyı ever had so many objections made to his obsequies. To the cemetery, near Parma, in November, 1876, the embalmed remains of Paganini were transposed from the family villa at Gaione, by order of his son, the Baron Achille (who died in December, 1895). The funeral was held at night by torchlight. A nephew, the Baron Attila Paganini, followed, and crowds of curious sightseers joined the procession. In 1893 there was erected the beautiful mausoleum which is now depicted from the only known photograph, taken expressly for THE STRAD. It bears this inscription :—

Qui riposano le ceneri
di Nicolò Paganini
Che traendo dal violino armonie divine
Scosse genio insuperabile tutta Europa
e cinse all'Italia,
Nuova sfolgorante corona.

Mente elettissima
Compose stupendamente in musica
Ammirato dai piu illustri maestri.

Cuore oltremodo generoso
donò largamente
ai parenti, agli artisti ai poveri.

Beneath this cupola of white marble, with its granite columns, may the ashes of Paganini rest in peace. His true remains—his reputation, his influence, his music, are with us for ever.

Plate 14—Facing page 90.

PAGANINI IN PRISON. One of the many scandals which is contradicted in the text. (See page 90.) There is another prison story that during Paganini's incarceration, he was reduced to the G, in consequence of the other strings having broken—hence his wonderful development of the fourth. This is again apocryphal. Paganini has greater claim to a scientific knowledge of the acoustical property of strings.

Plates 15, 16, and 17, see pages 101, 102, and 103,

are reproductions of Paganini's MSS. in the British Museum. No. 15, a letter (dated April 16th, 1832, and in French) thanking the person addressed, for kindness shown to his " cher fils Achille," Nos. 16 (dated February 19th, 1835) and 17 (dated May 5th, 1838); short notes (in Italian) are interesting autographs. Paganini was proverbially a " silent man "—his epistles are very rare.

Plates 18, 19, 20, 21, and 22—Pages 129-133.

These reproductions of rare programmes tell their own tales—they are interesting, because there are seen the items and the arrangement of concerts, also the prices, for admission, etc.—in those years.

Plate 23—Facing page 136.

FACSIMILE OF A LETTER BY PAGANINI, dated 1829. It was formerly in the possession of the late Mr. Carrodus, the great English violinist.

Plate 24— Facing page 144.

A SEMI-CARICATURE OF PAGANINI with the inscription.

The Modern Apollo (not Belvedere)
Receiving the homage of 5,000 persons, after having pocketed
£2,000 for two hours peformance.

Sketched at his last Concert at the King's Theatre. Published by G. Madeley, Wellington Street, Strand, 1831.

Plates 25 and 26, see pages 176 and 177.

Reproductions of music MS. in British Museum. A Theme, with variations for violin, with accompaniment, is a curious example of the great master's compositions.

Plate 27—Facing page 190.

COPY OF A RARE COPPER MEDAL struck in Paganini's honor in 1831.

BIBLIOGRAPHY.

THE extraordinary career of Paganini has received more attention than the life of any other instrumentalist. Of these biographies, it is impossible to give a complete list.

The following may, however, be commended.

"Paganini in seinem Reisewagen und Zimmer, in seinen redseligen Stunden, in gesellsschaftlichen Kirkeln, und seinen Concerten." Brunswick, Vieweg, 1830. Mr. George Harris, the writer of this pamphlet, was an Englishman, who in order to study Paganini, became the Violinist's secretary and interpreter.

"Leben, Charakter und Kunst N. Paganini's—Eine Skizze,"—by M. F. Shütz, a Professor at Halle. Leipzig, 1830.

"Paganini's Leben und Treiben als Künstler und als Mensch." Prague, 1830. Written by Professor Schottky.

"Paganini's Leben und Charakter," by M. L. Vinela. Hamburg, 1830.

"Notice sur le célèbre violoniste Nicolò Paganini," by M. J. Imbert de Laphaléque. Paris.

" Paganini et de Bériot, ou Avis aux artistes qui se
    destinent à l'enseignement du Violon," by F. Fayolle.
    Paris, 1831.

" Paganini, his life, his person, and a few words upon his
    secret," by J. L. Anders.   Paris, 1831.

" Vita di Nicolò Paganini di Genova, scritta ed illustrata
    da Giancarlo Conestabile, socio di varie Academie."
    Perugia, 1831.

" Nicolo Paganini," by F. J. Fétis.   Published by
    Schott and Co.

" L'Album."   " Paganini."   Rome, 1840.

" Good Words."   Three articles by Rev. H. R. Haweis,
    M.A.

" Musical Gem."   " Paganini."   Portrait by R. J.
    Hamerton.   London, 1832.

" The Violin," with some account of that leading instru-
    ment and its most eminent professors, by George
    Dubourg, 1836 and 1878.   This interesting book
    contains a long account of Paganini (illustrated.)

" Life of Moscheles."   Two vols.   1873.   In Vol. I.,
    chapters 13 and 14, " Paganini."

" Louis Spohr's Autobiography," *vide* " Paganini,"
    Vol. I., page 279, and Vol. II., page 168.   Spohr
    says: "His (Paganini's) left hand and his constantly
    pure intonation were to me astonishing."

" Dictionary of Music and Musicians," by Sir George
    Grove, D.C.L., *vide* article Paganini.

" Encyclopädie der gesammten musicalischen Wissens-chaften," by Dr. Gustav Schilling. Article Paganini.

Dr. Riemann's " Dictionary of Music," article Paganini.

" The Strad," various articles and paragraphs in the series of this journal.

" The Violin," by George Hart. Engravings of Paganini's Violin.

" Old Violins and their Makers," by James M. Fleming.

" Ole Bull," by Sara C. Bull.   Various notices of Paganini.

" Musical Opinion," July, August, and September, 1888. A renowned fiddler (Paganini.)   Three articles by Richard Harrison.

" Musical News," 1903.

" A Wooden Shoe" (Story of Paganini) by M. P. Audebrand.

" Paganiniana," (circa 1865.)

" Troubadour," August, 1899.   Paganini, by Richard Harrison.

" The Athenæum," 1831.   Critiques on Paganini.

" The Tatler," 1831.

" An account of Paganini's début in London," June 3rd, 1831, by Mr. Gardner of Leicester, appears in Dubourg's " Violin."

" Paganini's Concerts in Paris."   A clever description was published in " Le Globe."

" Foreign Quarterly Review " (circa 1832).

" Catalogue of Paganini's compositions," by M. Conestabile.

Paganini's works are published by Ricordi and Co., of Milan, and Schott and Co., of Mayence and London.

" Revue et Gazette Musicale de Paris," December 23rd, 1840. Article Paganini.

" Story of the Violin," by Paul Stoeving.

" The Quarterly Musical Magazine and Review," Vol. X.

" Ueber Paganini's Kunst, die Violine zu spielen," by Carl F. W. Guhr, original edition 1831. Modern. Schott and Co.

" Biographical Sketches of Celebrated Violinists." London : Bentley, publisher.

" Celebrated Violinists, Past and Present." Translated from the German of A. Ehrlich, and edited with notes and additions by Robin H. Legge (eighteen pages devoted to Paganini). Portraits. STRAD Office, London.

" Notice of Antony Stradivari," by F. J. Fétis. Translated by John Bishop. London, 1864.

" The Harmonicon." An excellent musical journal. Published in London (contemporary with Paganini).

" The Life of Rossini," by Sutherland Edwards.

" History of Music," by Emil Naumann. 2 vols. Cassell and Co., London, 1886.

" Life and Letters of Sir Charles Hallé." Paganini is mentioned by a musical amateur (Count de Stendhal), 1814 and 1817.

" Diary of an Invalid," by Mathews, 1818.

" History of the Violin," by William Sandys and S. A. Forster, 1864.

" Old Violins," by Rev. H. R. Haweis, M.A. 1898.

" Researches into the History of the Violin Family," by Carl Engel. 1883.

" Musical World." 1836.

" Musical and Personal Recollections," by Henry Phillips, 1864.

" Music and Manners in France and Germany," by Henry F. Chorley. 1841.

" The Student's History of Music," by F. L. Ritter. 1880.

Collectors will be interested in the Medals and Busts of Paganini.

The English and Continental contemporary Press notices, etc., would alone make a Paganini volume.

Of Paganini, there are many portraits, though too generally caricatures. M. Fétis, in his Life of Paganini, gives a short but incomplete catalogue. Those included in this volume have been carefully selected from contemporary prints, etc.